T0043791

OXFORD PICTURE DICTIONARY

Content Areas for Kids

Workbook

Elizabeth Buckley

Program Consultant
Kate Kinsella

OXFORD
UNIVERSITY PRESS

OXFORD
UNIVERSITY PRESS

198 Madison Avenue
New York, NY 10016 USA

Great Clarendon Street, Oxford, OX2 6DP, United Kingdom

Oxford University Press is a department of the University of Oxford. It furthers the University's objective of excellence in research, scholarship, and education by publishing worldwide. Oxford is a registered trade mark of Oxford University Press in the UK and in certain other countries

© Oxford University Press 2012

The moral rights of the author have been asserted

First published in 2012
16 23

No unauthorized photocopying

All rights reserved. No part of this publication may be reproduced, stored in a retrieval system, or transmitted, in any form or by any means, without the prior permission in writing of Oxford University Press, or as expressly permitted by law, by licence or under terms agreed with the appropriate reprographics rights organization. Enquiries concerning reproduction outside the scope of the above should be sent to the ELT Rights Department, Oxford University Press, at the address above

You must not circulate this work in any other form and you must impose this same condition on any acquirer

Links to third party websites are provided by Oxford in good faith and for information only. Oxford disclaims any responsibility for the materials contained in any third party website referenced in this work

General Manager, American ELT: Laura Pearson
Publisher: Stephanie Karras
Development Editor: Kelley Perrella
Director, ADP: Susan Sanguily
Executive Design Manager: Maj-Britt Hagsted
Associate Design Manager: Michael Steinhofer
Designer: Sangeeta E. Ramcharan
Electronic Production Manager: Julie Armstrong
Production Artist: Elissa Santos
Image Manager: Trisha Masterson
Senior Image Editor: Fran Newman
Senior Manufacturing Controller: Eve Wong

ISBN: 978 0 19 401779 4

Printed in China
This book is printed on paper from certified and well-managed sources

ACKNOWLEDGEMENTS

Illustrations by: Lalena Fisher: 4, 7, 33; Aga Kowalska: 70, 71, 84, 85, 89, 115, 118, 119, 121, 139, 149, 153; Anthony Lewis: 18, 19, 21, 29, 41, 53, 66, 67, 77, 79, 92, 93; Julissa Mora: 16, 17, 27, 39, 44, 45, 57, 64, 65, 68, 69, 100, 101, 129, 133, 141, 143, 156, 157; Caroline Romanet: 12, 13, 24, 25, 37, 49, 60, 61, 97, 127, 147, 151; Anita Romeo: 22, 23, 31, 47, 51, 72, 73, 103, 131, 161, 167; Jamie Smith: 108, 109, 111, 112, 113, 117, 123; Jomike Tejido: 14, 15, 35, 43, 58, 59, 62, 63, 75, 83, 87, 94, 95, 98, 99, 107, 135, 144, 145, 158, 159, 163, 165. Additional illustrations sourced from: Oxford Picture Dictionary: Content Areas for Kids.

Cover Illustrator: Leslie Harrington

Cover Design: Sangeeta E. Ramcharan

Table of Contents

Getting Started

Numbers 2
Ordinals 4
Calendar 5
Time 6
Color 7
Opposites 8
Prepositions 10

Unit 1 At Home

1 Every Day 12
2 Friends 14
3 Family 16
4 Home 18
5 The Bedroom 20
6 The Bathroom 22
7 Breakfast in the Kitchen 24
8 The Living Room 26
9 Everyday Clothes 28
10 Seasonal Clothes 30
Unit Expansion: At Home 32

Unit 2 At School

11 A Day at School 34
12 The School 36
13 School Supplies 38
14 Classroom 40
15 The Library 42
16 The Computer Lab 44
17 Lunch in the Cafeteria 46
18 Physical Education 48
19 The Nurse's Office 50
20 Feelings 52
Unit Expansion: At School 54

Unit 3 Community

21 People at Work 56
22 The Neighborhood 58
23 The Community 60
24 Businesses in Town 62
25 The Supermarket 64
26 The Restaurant 66
27 The City 68
28 Transportation 70
29 The Harbor 72
30 The Hospital 74
31 Fire Safety 76
32 The Farm 78
Unit Expansion: Community 80

Unit 4 The United States

33 Biography Verbs 82

34 Map Skills 84

35 The Government 86

36 American Symbols 88

Unit Expansion: The United States 90

Unit 5 Health

37 Healthy Habits 92

38 Faces 94

39 Parts of the Body 96

40 More Parts of the Body 98

41 The Senses 100

42 Nutrition 102

Unit Expansion: Health 104

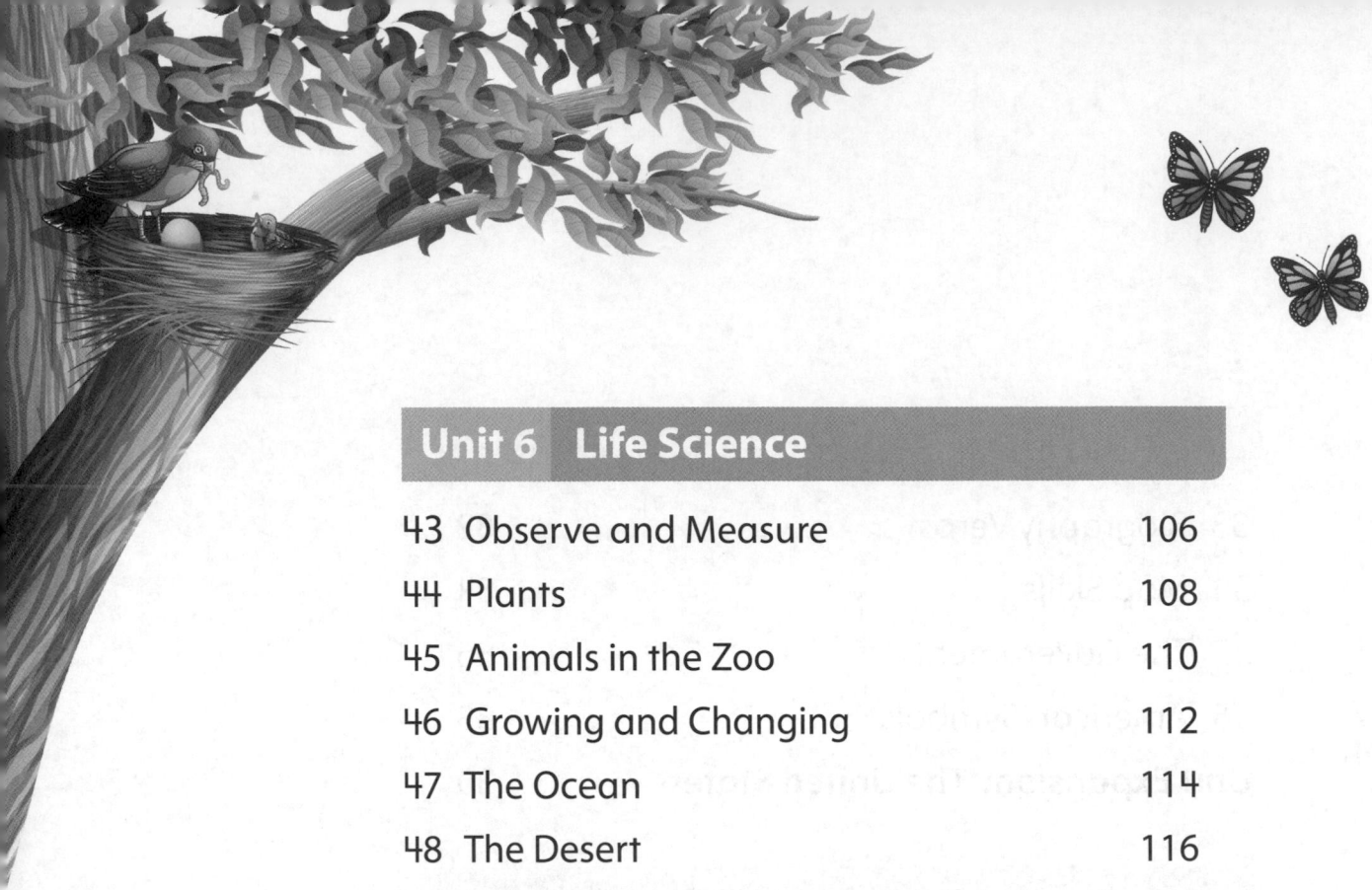

Unit 6 Life Science

43 Observe and Measure 106

44 Plants 108

45 Animals in the Zoo 110

46 Growing and Changing 112

47 The Ocean 114

48 The Desert 116

49 The Forest 118

50 The Rain Forest 120

51 The Grassland 122

Unit Expansion: Life Science 124

Unit 7 Physical Science

52 Experiment and Record 126

53 Matter 128

54 Heat, Light, and Sound 130

55 Motion and Force 132

56 Energy and Electricity 134

Unit Expansion: Physical Science 136

Unit 8 Earth and Space Science

57 Land and Water 138

58 In the Mountains 140

59 Earth Materials 142

60 Dinosaurs and Fossils 144

61 Weather 146

62 On the Coast 148

63 The Environment 150

64 Space 152

Unit Expansion: Earth and Space Science 154

Unit 9 Math

65 Telling Time 156

66 Math Words 158

67 Shapes 160

68 Fractions and Decimals 162

69 Measurement 164

70 Money 166

Unit Expansion: Math 168

Numbers

A Label.

eighteen	eleven	five	fifteen	four
thirteen	seven	twelve	twenty	two

	1	2	3	4
1.	one	_____	three	_____
	5	6	7	8
2.	_____	six	_____	eight
	9	10	11	12
3.	nine	ten	_____	_____
	13	14	15	16
4.	_____	fourteen	_____	sixteen
	17	18	19	20
5.	seventeen	_____	nineteen	_____

B Match.

1. eighty- - - -	100
2. twenty-three	29
3. one hundred	96
4. eighty-eight	23
5. twenty-four	24
6. twenty-nine	80
7. ninety-six	88
8. twenty-five	25

C Label.

thirty seventy fifty

1. _____ 2. _____ 3. _____

Ordinal Numbers

A Label.

fifth tenth first fourth second eighth

1. _____

2. _____

3. _____

4. _____

5. _____

6. _____

B Label.

6th 7th 9th 3rd

1st 2nd _____ 4th 5th _____ _____ 8th _____ 10th

Calendar

A Label.

December July May March January October

_____						
1	2	3	4	5	6	7
8	9	10	11	12	13	14
15	16	17	18	19	20	21
22	23	24	25	26	27	28
29	30	31				

February						
			1	2	3	4
5	6	7	8	9	10	11
12	13	14	15	16	17	18
19	20	21	22	23	24	25
26	27	28	29			

_____						
			1	2	3	
4	5	6	7	8	9	10
11	12	13	14	15	16	17
18	19	20	21	22	23	24
25	26	27	28	29	30	31

April						
1	2	3	4	5	6	7
8	9	10	11	12	13	14
15	16	17	18	19	20	21
22	23	24	25	26	27	28
29	30					

_____						
		1	2	3	4	5
6	7	8	9	10	11	12
13	14	15	16	17	18	19
20	21	22	23	24	25	26
27	28	29	30	31		

June						
					1	2
3	4	5	6	7	8	9
10	11	12	13	14	15	16
17	18	19	20	21	22	23
24	25	26	27	28	29	30

_____						
1	2	3	4	5	6	7
8	9	10	11	12	13	14
15	16	17	18	19	20	21
22	23	24	25	26	27	28
29	30	31				

August						
		1	2	3	4	
5	6	7	8	9	10	11
12	13	14	15	16	17	18
19	20	21	22	23	24	25
26	27	28	29	30	31	

September						
						1
2	3	4	5	6	7	8
9	10	11	12	13	14	15
16	17	18	19	20	21	22
23	24	25	26	27	28	29
30						

_____						
	1	2	3	4	5	6
7	8	9	10	11	12	13
14	15	16	17	18	19	20
21	22	23	24	25	26	27
28	29	30	31			

November						
				1	2	3
4	5	6	7	8	9	10
11	12	13	14	15	16	17
17	19	20	21	22	23	24
25	26	27	28	29	30	

_____						
						1
2	3	4	5	6	7	8
9	10	11	12	13	14	15
16	17	18	19	20	21	22
23	24	25	26	27	28	29
30	31					

B Write the days in the correct order.

Thursday Wednesday Friday Monday Saturday Tuesday

1. Sunday _____
2. _____
3. _____
4. _____
5. _____
6. _____
7. _____

Time

A Label.

afternoon evening midnight morning night noon

1. _____

2. _____

3. _____

4. _____

5. _____

6. _____

Colors

A Color.

1. 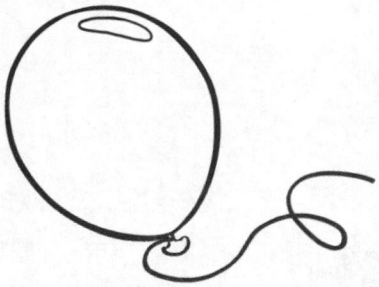

blue

2. 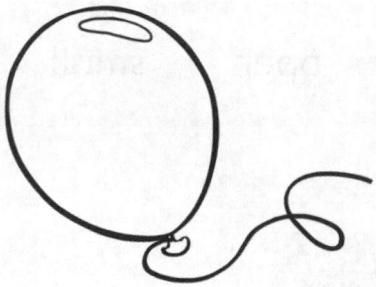

pink

3. 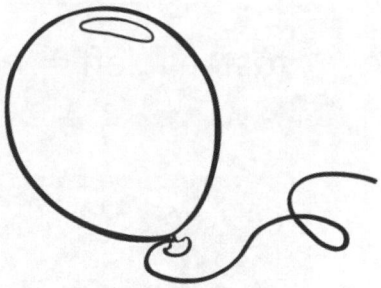

brown

4. 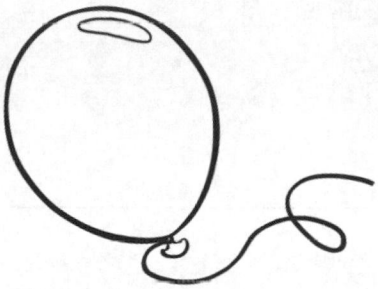

black

5. 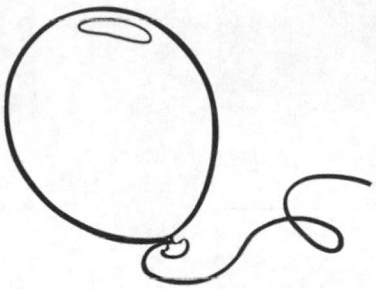

purple

6. 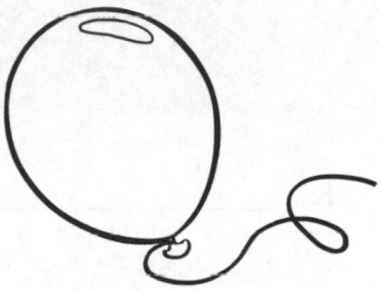

white

7. 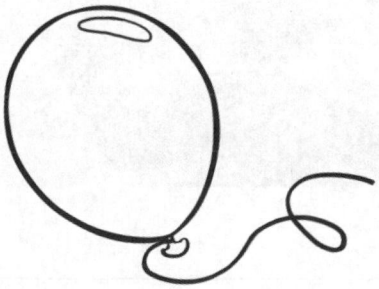

green

8. 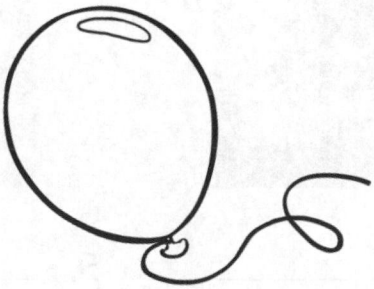

red

9. 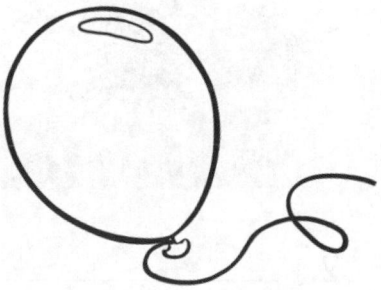

tan

10. 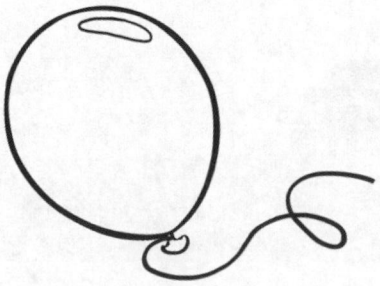

orange

11. 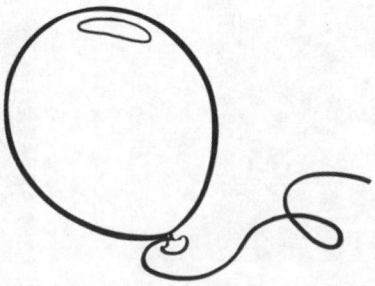

yellow

12. 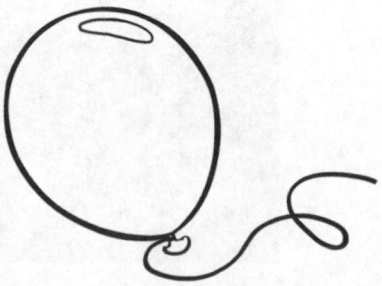

gray

Opposites

A Label.

fast left new open small tall

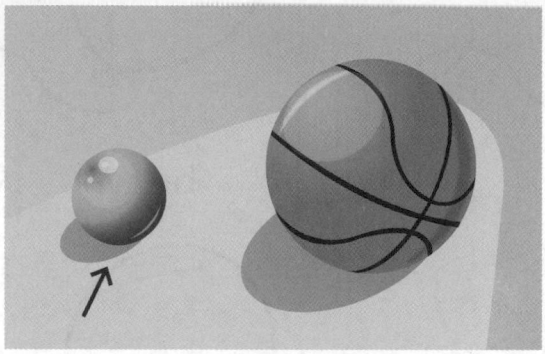

1. _____

2. _____

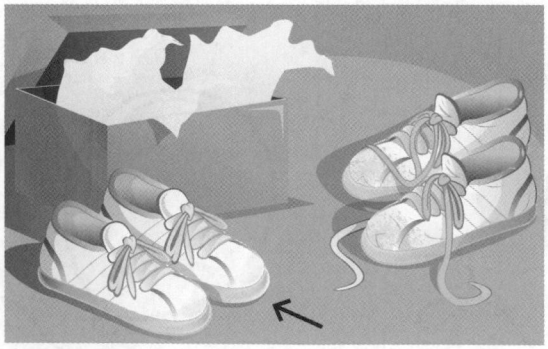

3. _____

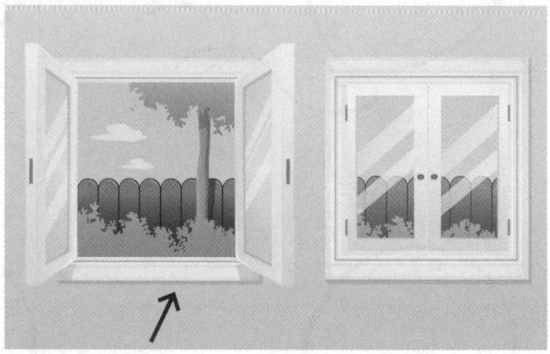

4. _____

5. _____

6. _____

B Write.

cold different dirty empty heavy wet

1. Full is the opposite of _____.

2. Light is the opposite of _____.

3. Clean is the opposite of _____.

4. Dry is the opposite of _____.

5. Hot is the opposite of _____.

6. Same is the opposite of _____.

Prepositions

A Circle.

1. The book is (between) next to the boxes.

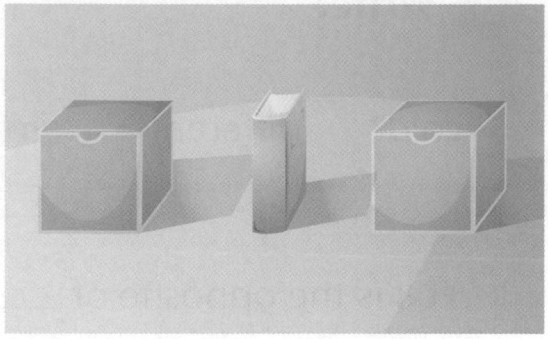

2. The girl goes up down the stairs.

3. The girl goes around through the tree.

4. The book is on in the box.

B Write.

above behind across from in front of over below under

1. The girl is _____ the boy.

2. The clock is _____ the ball.

   The ball is _____ the clock.

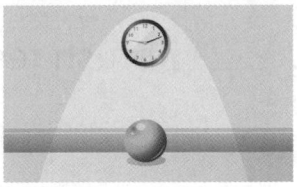

3. The car goes _____ the bridge.

   The boat goes _____ the bridge.

4. The girl is _____ the boy.

   The boy is _____ the girl.

1 Every Day

A Match.

1. _____ comb hair
2. _____ get dressed
3. _____ eat breakfast
4. _____ brush teeth

a.

b.

c.

d.

B Write.

eats takes wakes

1. He _____ up.

2. He _____ a shower

3. She _____ dinner.

C Write.

takes a bath does homework goes to bed

1. She _____ at 6:30 p.m.

2. He _____ at 7:30 p.m.

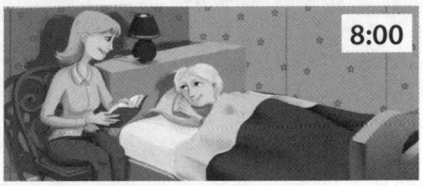

3. She _____ at 8:00 p.m.

D Look at the pictures. Write.

1. She _____ up at 7:00 a.m.

2. She _____.

3. _____.

2 Friends

A Match.

1. _____ bangs
2. _____ glasses
3. _____ eyelashes
4. _____ ponytail
5. _____ eye
6. _____ hair

B Match.

dark short straight long curly light

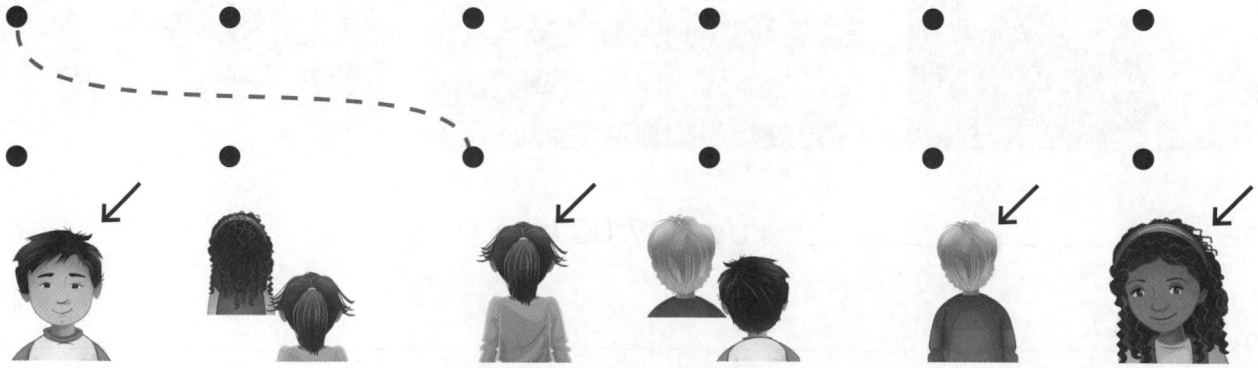

C Write.

1. She has _____ eyes.

2. He has short, _____ hair.

3. She has _____, curly hair.

D Look at the picture. Write.

1. Emma has long, _____ hair.

2. Ted has _____, _____.

3. Mary _____.

3 Family

A Label.

grandmother	grandfather	mother	father
sister	brother	aunt	uncle

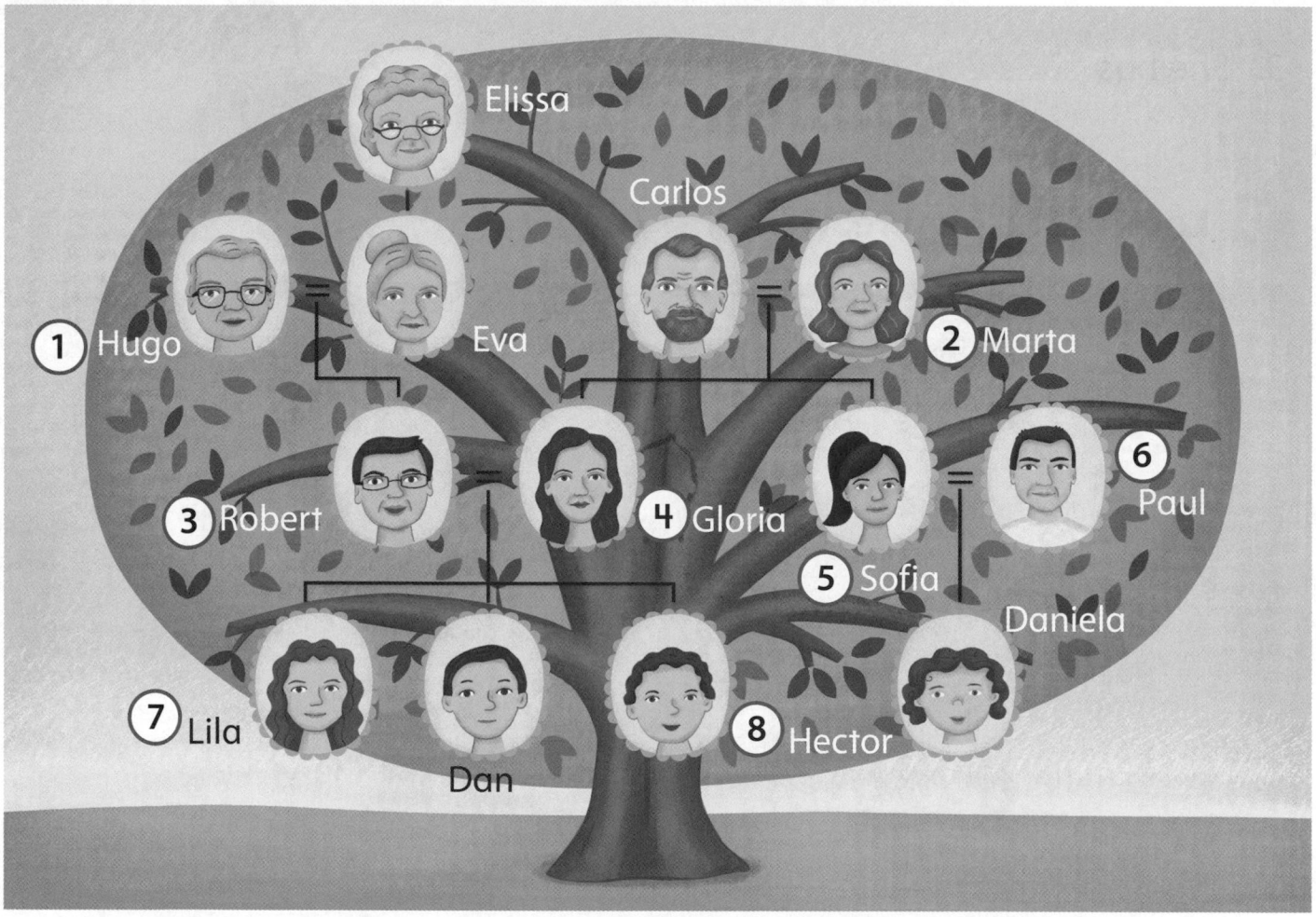

1. _____
2. _____
3. _____
4. _____
5. _____
6. _____
7. _____
8. _____

B Look at Dan's family tree on page 16. Write.

parents cousin great-grandmother grandparents

1. Daniela is his _____.
2. Elissa is his _____.
3. Hugo and Eva are his _____.
4. Gloria and Robert are his _____.

C Look at the picture. Write.

1. Lila is Dan's _____.
2. Carlos and Marta are his _____.
3. Sofia and Paul _____.

4 Home

A Match.

1. _____ cook
2. _____ wall
3. _____ eat
4. _____ floor
5. _____ stairs
6. _____ window
7. _____ table
8. _____ sink
9. _____ door
10. _____ cabinet

B Write.

1. There is a _____.

2. There are two _____.

3. There are three _____.

C Look at the picture. Write.

1. There _____ stairs.

2. There are three _____.

3. There _____.

5 The Bedroom

A Write.

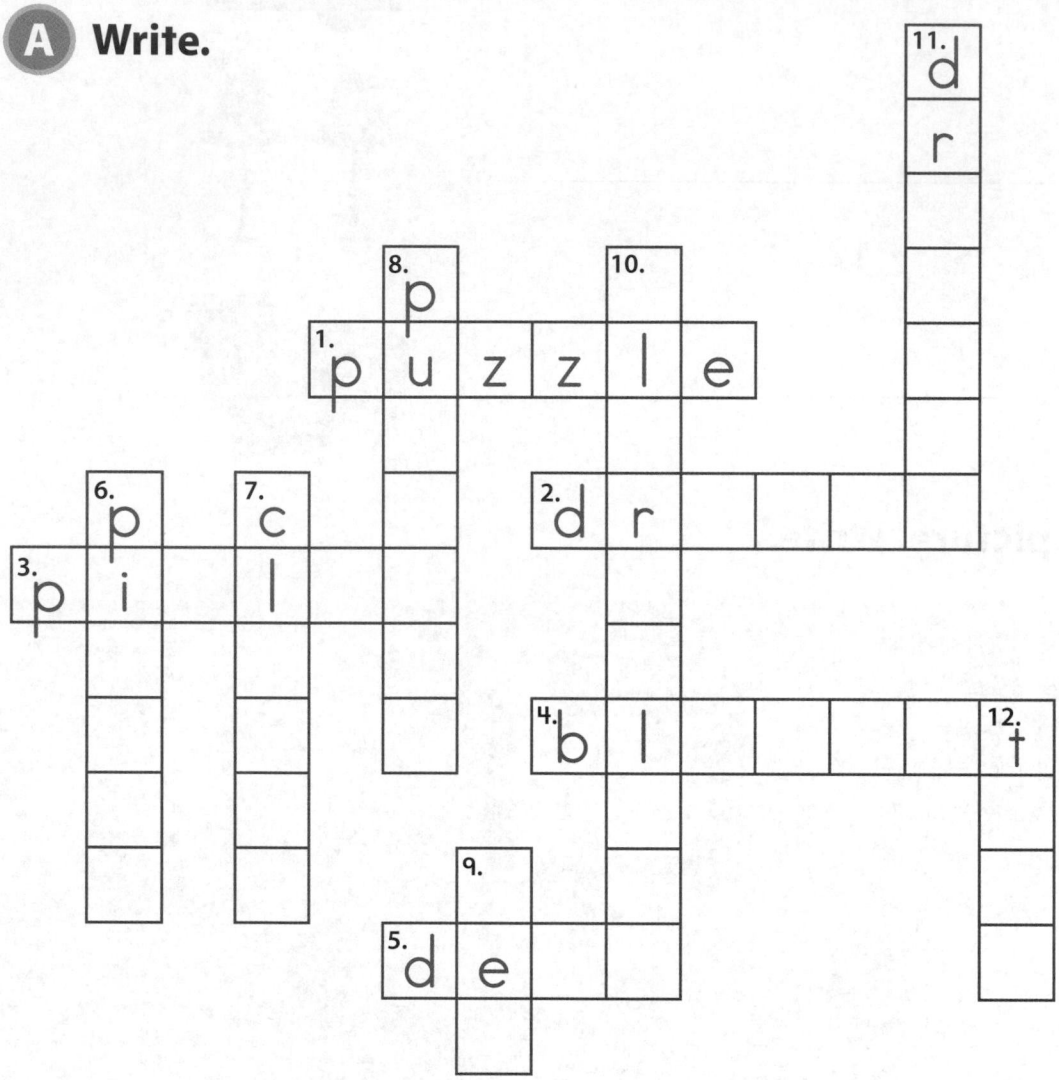

Across

1. 
2. 
3. 
4. 
5. 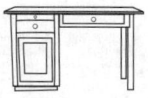

Down

6. 
7. 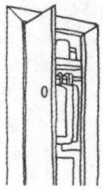
8. 
9. 
10. 

11. 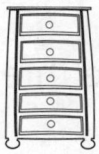
12. 

B Write *in, on,* or *under.*

1. The puzzle is _____ the drawer.

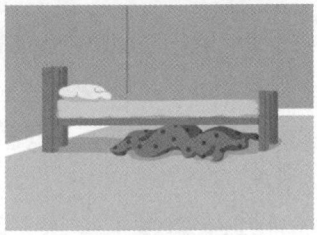

2. The blanket is _____ the bed.

3. The alarm clock is _____ the desk.

C Look at the picture. Write.

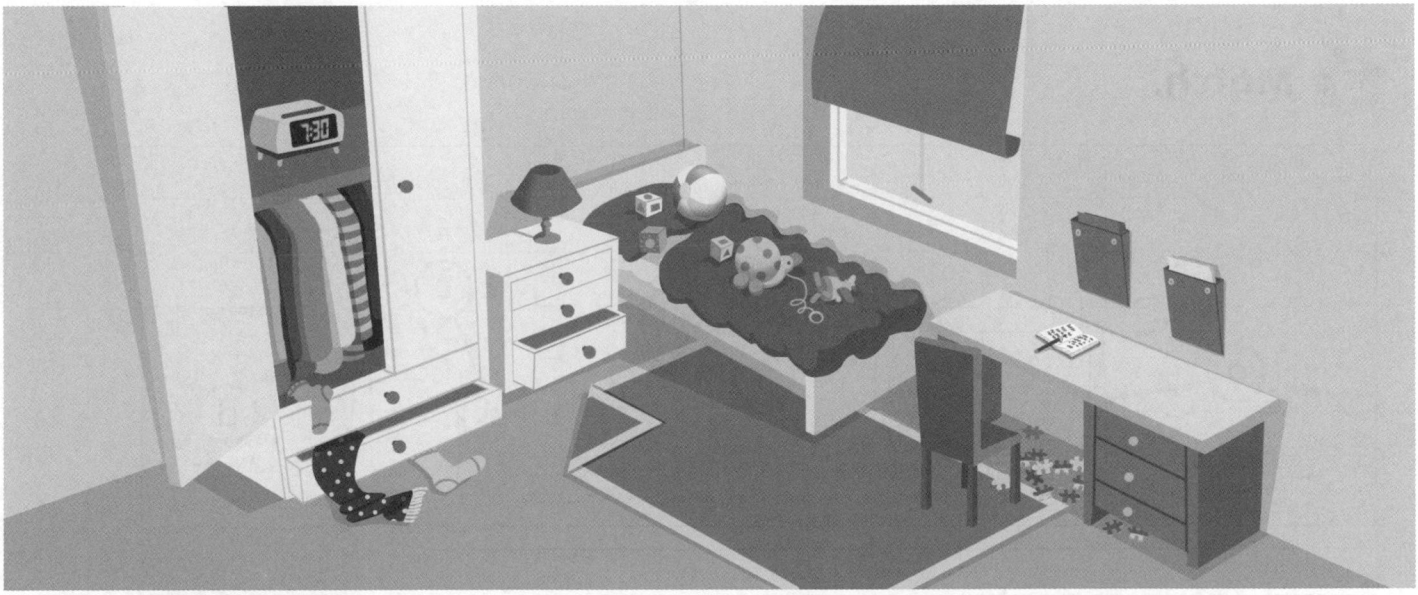

1. The toys are on the _____.
2. The puzzle _____.
3. The alarm clock _____.

6 The Bathroom

A Write.

1. c_____ _____ _____

3. _____ _____ _____ _____ _____paste

2. t_____ _____ _____ _____ _____

4. tooth_____ _____ _____ _____ _____

B Match.

1. _____ water
2. _____ shampoo
3. _____ bathtub
4. _____ soap
5. _____ towel

C Write.

washes brushes dries

1. She _____ her hands with a towel.

2. He _____ his hands with soap.

3. She _____ her teeth with a toothbrush.

D Look at the pictures. Write.

1. Tom washes his hair with _____.

2. He dries his hair with a _____.

3. _____.

7 Breakfast in the Kitchen

A Match.

1. _____ stove
2. _____ cabinet
3. _____ refrigerator
4. _____ cup
5. _____ counter
6. _____ plate

B Match.

butter ● ● cereal ● ● eggs ● ● bananas ● ● bread ● ● grapes ● ●

C Write.

1. Where is the _____?

   It's on the table.

2. Where are the _____?

   They're on the plate.

3. Where are the _____?

   They're on the counter.

D Look at the picture. Write.

1. The milk is on the _____.

2. The bread is _____.

3. The cereal _____.

8 The Living Room

A Circle the correct word.

1. 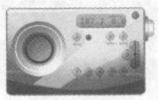

phone radio

2. 

sofa rug

3. 

rug sofa

4. 

television rug

5. 

remote telephone

6. 

television remote

B Label.

play talk help

1. _____ 2. _____ 3. _____

C Write.

helping talking studying

1. He's _____ the boy.

2. She's _____.

3. He's _____ on the phone.

D Look at the picture. Write.

1. They're _____ a game.

2. He's _____.

3. He's _____.

9 Everyday Clothes

A Match.

1. _____ pants
2. _____ sneakers
3. _____ underwear
4. _____ baseball cap
5. _____ skirt
6. _____ shoes
7. _____ dress
8. _____ socks
9. _____ sweatshirt
10. _____ pajamas

a.

b.

c.

d.

e.

f.

g.

h.

i.

j.

B Write. Then color.

1. What color is the _____?

   It's red.

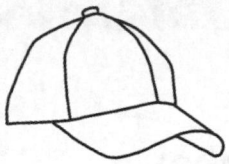

2. What color are the _____?

   They're blue.

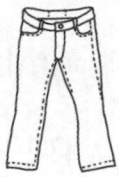

3. What color is the _____?

   It's yellow.

C Color the picture. Then write.

1. The socks are _____.

2. The sweatshirt is _____.

3. _____.

10 Seasonal Clothes

A Label.

jacket	umbrella	bathing suit	sandals	scarf	gloves
T-shirt	pants	shorts	sunglasses	raincoat	boots

Spring	Summer	Fall	Winter
_____	_____	_____	_____
_____	_____	_____	_____
_____	_____	_____	_____

B Write.

1. He's wearing _____

   and a _____.

2. She's wearing a _____

   and _____.

3. They're wearing _____.

C Look at the picture. Write.

1. They're wearing rain _____.

2. They're wearing _____.

3. _____.

A Match.

1. _____ bed

2. _____ refrigerator

3. _____ sink

4. _____ sofa

5. _____ window

a. 

b. 

c. 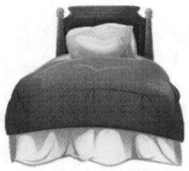

d. 

e. 

B Look at the chart on page 32 in the *Dictionary*. Write.

1. There is a _____ and a window in the bedroom.

2. There is a _____ and a window in the living room.

3. There is a _____ and a _____ in the bathroom.

4. There is a _____, _____, and a _____ in the kitchen.

C Complete the chart.

The Home				
	kitchen	living room	bedroom	bathroom
table	✗			
dresser				
shower				
stove				
mirror				

D Look at your chart in C. Write.

1. There is a dresser in the _____.

2. There is a shower and a _____ in the _____.

3. There is a _____ and a _____ _____.

4. _____ _____.

11 A Day at School

A Label.

raise	read	write	draw
repeat	work	answer	think

1. _____

2. _____

3. _____

4. _____ questions

5. _____

6. _____

7. _____ hand

8. _____ with a partner

B Write.

asks reads works

1. What does he do at school?

   He _____.

2. What does she do at school?

   She _____ questions.

3. What does he do at school?

   He _____ in a group.

C Look at the picture. Write.

1. Carlos _____ at school.

2. Jun listens and _____.

3. Amy _____.

12 The School

A Write.

1. l___ ibrarian

2. ___ afeteria worker

3. t ___ ___ ___ ___ ___ ___

4. ___ ___ ___ driver

5. ___ ecretary

6. ___ ___ ossing guard

7. c ___ ___ ___ ___ ___ ___ ___ ___

8. n ___ ___ ___ ___

B Answer the questions.

principal	classroom	student
office	teacher's aide	

1. Where is the _____?

   She's in the classroom.

2. Where is the _____?

   She's in the _____.

3. Where are the teacher and the _____?

   They're in the _____.

C Look at the pictures. Write.

1. The cafeteria worker is in the _____.
2. The students are _____.
3. The coach _____.

13 School Supplies

A Match.

1. _____ crayon
2. _____ pencil
3. _____ eraser
4. _____ pen
5. _____ pencil sharpener
6. _____ calculator
7. _____ book
8. _____ binder
9. _____ scissors
10. _____ marker
11. _____ backpack

a.

b.

c.

d.

e.

f.

g.

h.

i.

j.

k.

B Write.

1. He has two _____.

2. She has three _____.

3. They have six _____.

C Look at the picture. Write.

1. They have scissors and _____.

2. She has eight _____.

3. He _____.

14 The Classroom

A Circle the correct word.

1. 

globe chair

2. 

glue notebook

3. 

map clock

4. 

tape board

5. 

board glue

6. 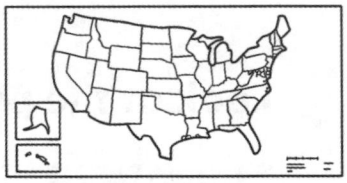

flag map

7. 

ruler trash can

8. 

notebook globe

9. 

tape flag

10. 

paper ruler

11. 

trash can map

12. 

glue notebook

B Write *in* or *on*.

1. The paper is _____ the trash can.

2. The map is _____ the board.

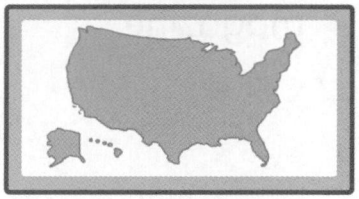

3. The globe is _____ the desk.

C Look at the picture. Write.

1. The books are on the _____.

2. The map is _____.

3. The paper _____.

15 The Library

A Match.

magazine ● ●

newspaper ● ●

atlas ● ●

dictionary ● ●

DVD ● ●

B Write.

bookshelves	call number	catalog	return	card

1. Look in the _____.

2. Go to the _____.

3. Look at the _____.

4. Give the librarian your library _____.

5. Don't forget to _____ the book on time!

C Write.

checking out looking returning

1. They're _____ a DVD.

2. She's _____ a book.

3. He's _____ at a magazine.

D Look at the picture. Write.

1. He's checking out a _____.

2. She's _____ a DVD.

3. They're _____.

16 The Computer Lab

A Label.

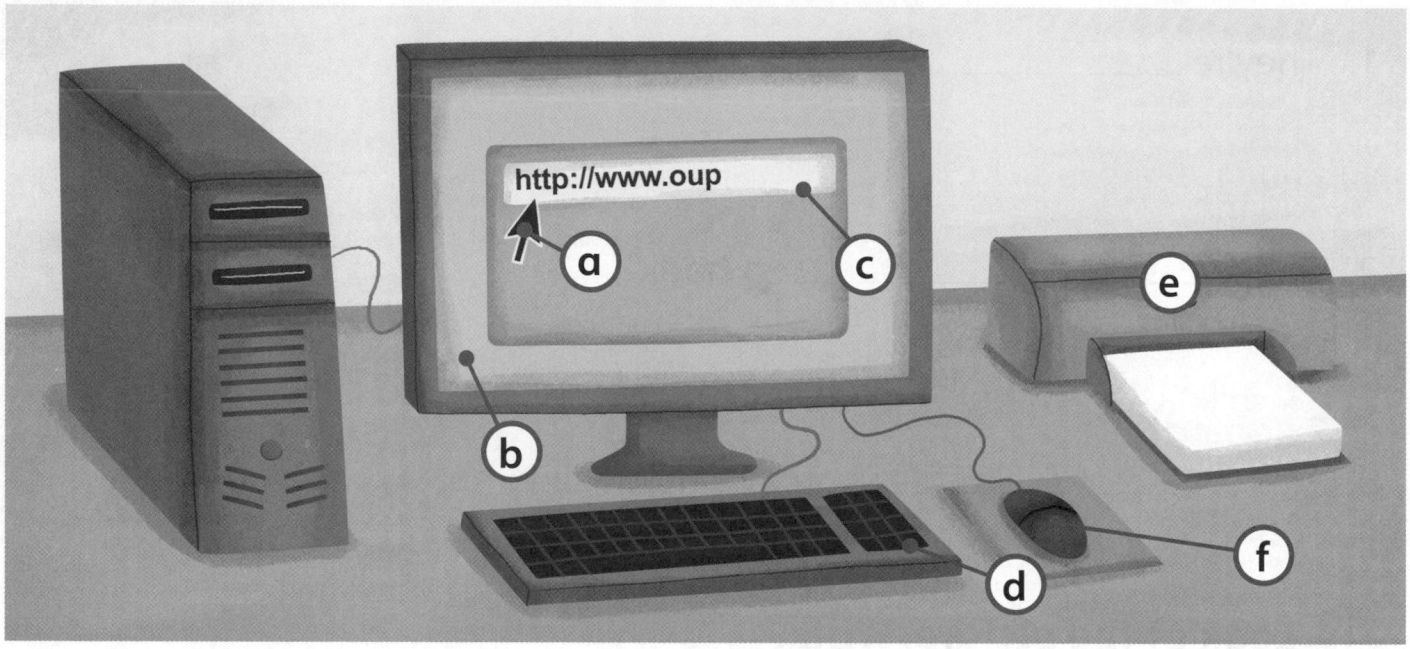

1. _____ printer
2. _____ monitor
3. _____ Internet
4. _____ keyboard
5. _____ mouse
6. _____ cursor

B Write.

click type log in

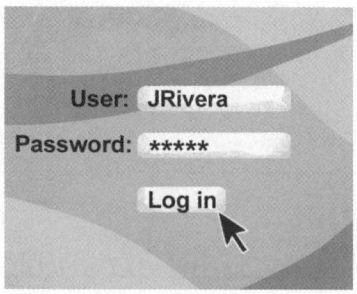

1. _____
2. _____
3. _____

C Write.

headset computers microphone

1. She's using a _____.
2. He's using a _____.
3. They're using _____.

D Look at the picture. Write.

1. Felix is using a _____.
2. Sam is _____.
3. Yuko _____.

17 Lunch in the Cafeteria

A Match.

sandwich • juice • strawberries • carrots • crackers • milk •

• • • • • •

B Write.

tray bag carton bottle

1. a _____ of milk

2. a _____ of carrots

3. a _____ of juice

4. a _____ of food

C Write.

1. He has a can of _____.

2. She has a _____ of _____.

3. She has a _____ of _____.

D Look at the picture. Write.

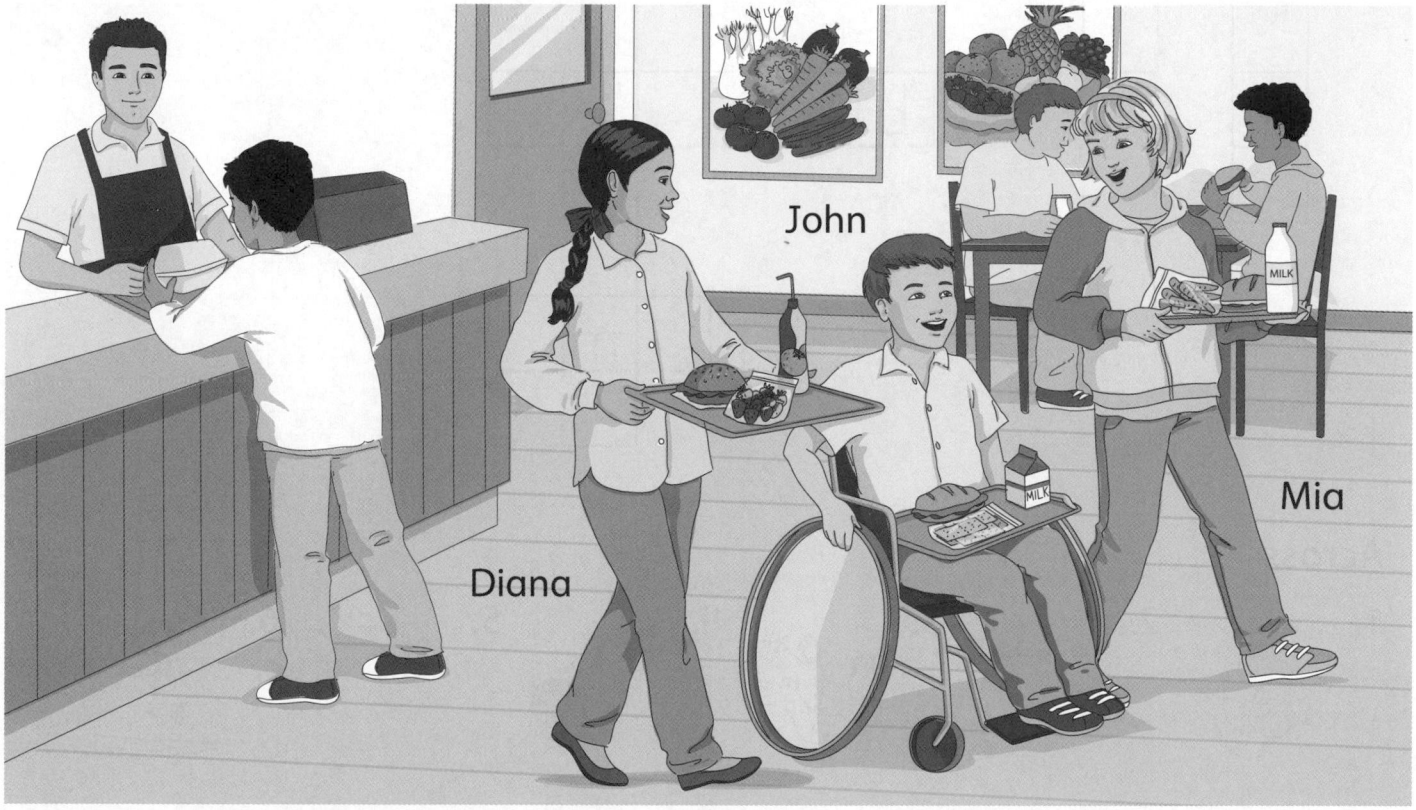

1. Diana has a bottle of juice and a bag of _____.

2. John has a carton of _____.

3. Mia _____.

18 Physical Education

A Write.

Across

1. 
2. 
3. 
4. 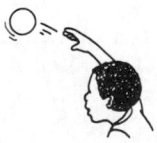
5. 
6. 

Down

7. 
8. 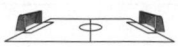
9. 
10. 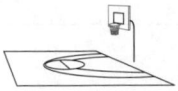
11. 
12. 

B Write.

catches kicks throws

1. He _____ the ball.

2. She _____ the ball.

3. She _____ the ball.

C Look at the picture. Write.

1. Kathy _____ on the court.

2. David _____ on the court.

3. Yaminah _____.

19 The Nurse's Office

A Match.

1. _____ bandage
2. _____ cut
3. _____ fever
4. _____ thermometer
5. _____ sore throat
6. _____ tissues

a.

b.

c.

d.

e.

f.

B Write.

bleed lay down cough sneeze

1. _____

2. _____

3. _____

4. _____

C Answer the questions.

earache fever stomachache

1. What's the matter with Jenny?

   She has a _____.

2. What's the matter with Mark?

   He has an _____.

3. What's the matter with Clara?

   She has a _____.

D Look at the picture. Write.

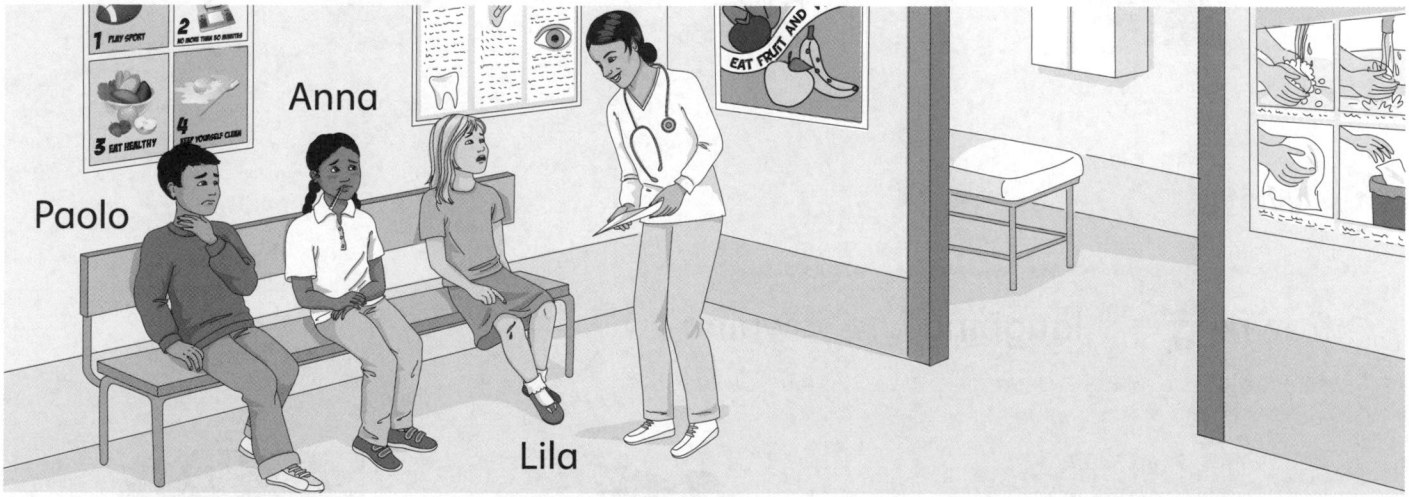

1. Lila has a _____.

2. Anna has _____.

3. Paolo _____.

20 Feelings

A Match.

scared tired angry happy sad surprised confused

B Write.

frowning laughing yawning

1. He's _____.
2. She's _____.
3. He's _____.

C Write.

1. He feels _____.

   He's _____.

2. He feels _____.

   He's _____.

3. She feels _____.

   She's _____.

D Look at the picture. Write.

1. The bus driver is _____. He feels _____.

2. The girl is _____. She _____.

3. The boy is _____. _____.

A Label.

ask draw climb kick read run smile type

1.  _____

2.  _____

3.  _____

4.  _____

5.  _____ questions

6.  _____

7.  _____

8.  _____

B Look at the chart on page 54 of the *Dictionary*. Write.

1. Students read, _____, and draw in the classroom.
2. Students run, _____, and _____ in the gym.
3. Students _____ and _____ in the classroom and the gym.

C Complete the Venn diagram.

bounce click jump laugh log in think throw write

In the Classroom

In the Gym

_____

_____

_____

_____

_____

_____

_____

_____

D Look at your Venn diagram in C. Write.

1. Students _____ in the classroom and the gym.
2. Students _____ a ball in the _____.
3. Students don't _____ a ball in the _____.
4. Students _____ and _____ in the gym.
5. _____

_____.

21 People at Work

A Match.

1. _____ build houses
2. _____ deliver mail
3. _____ protect the community
4. _____ fix cars
5. _____ sell clothes
6. _____ serve food
7. _____ fight fires
8. _____ grow crops
9. _____ raise animals
10. _____ take care of people

a.

b.

c.

d.

e.

f.

g.

h.

i.

j.

B Write.

1. What does he _____?

   He sells _____.

2. What does she _____?

   She serves _____.

3. What does he _____?

   He fixes _____.

C Look at the picture. Write.

1. She's a mail carrier. She delivers the _____.
2. He's a police officer. He _____.
3. She's a _____. _____.

22 The Neighborhood

A Match.

1. ____ street
2. ____ fence
3. ____ house
4. ____ streetlight
5. ____ address
6. ____ sidewalk
7. ____ street sign
8. ____ apartment building

B Look at A. Write *on* or *in*.

1. There's a stop sign _____ the corner.

2. There's a park _____ the street.

3. There's a bench _____ the park.

C Look at the picture. Write.

1. There are children in the _____.

2. There's a mother and baby on _____.

3. There's a father and _____.

23 The Community

A Write.

intersection	traffic light	crosswalk	taxi
mailbox	post office	cross the street	museum

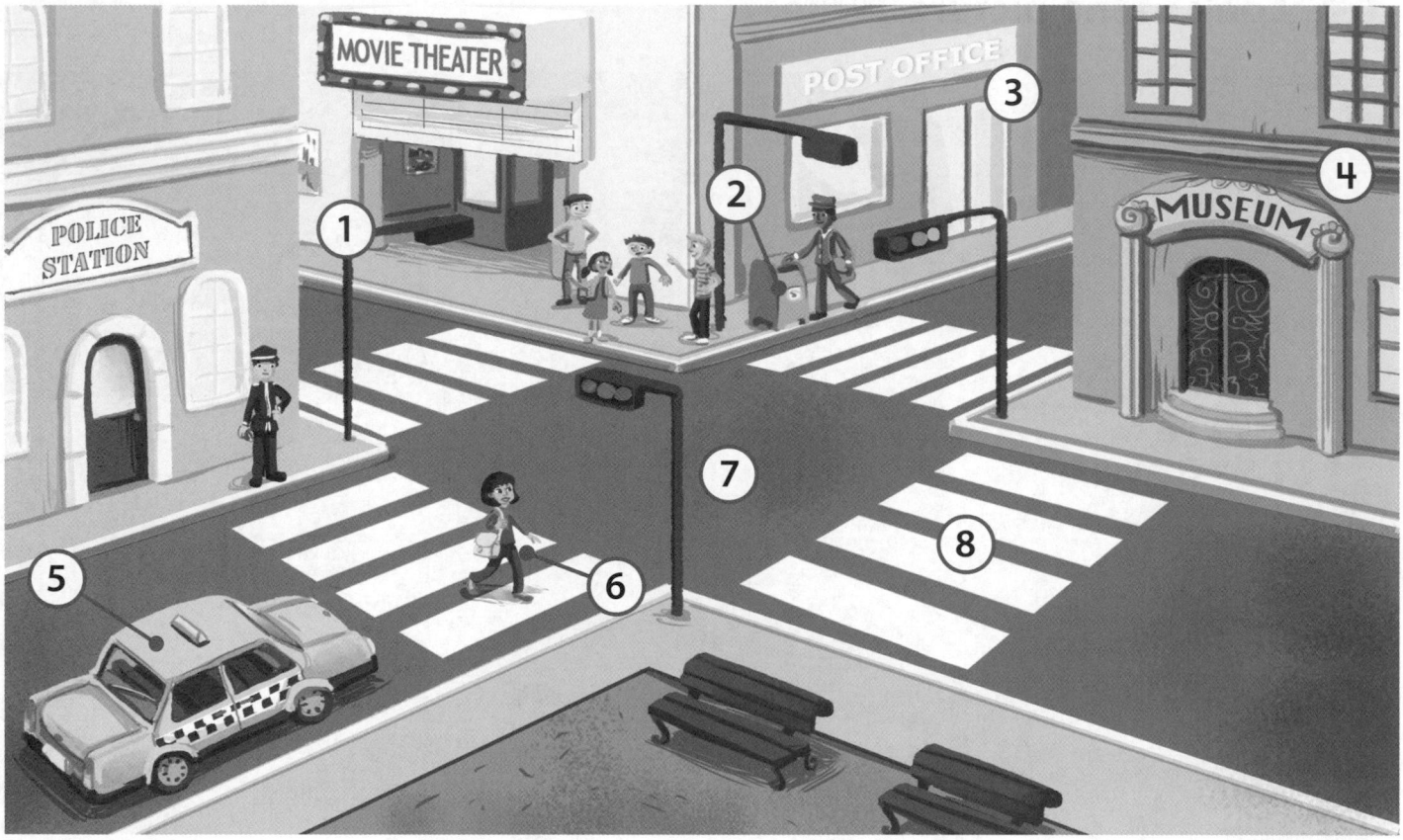

1. _____
2. _____
3. _____
4. _____
5. _____
6. _____
7. _____
8. _____

B Look at A. Write.

1. Where is the police officer?

   He's next to the _____.

2. Where is the mail carrier?

   He's next to the _____.

3. Where are the children?

   They're next to the _____.

C Look at the picture. Write.

1. The movie theater is next to the _____.

2. The park is _____.

3. The museum is _____.

24 Businesses in Town

A Where does each person work? Match.

pharmacist ●

cashier ●

salesperson ●

teller ●

● bank

● shoe store

● drugstore

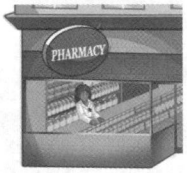

● supermarket

B Write.

gas station supermarket laundry

1. A customer at the _____ gets clean clothes.

2. A customer at the _____ gets gas.

3. A customer at the _____ gets groceries.

C Write.

bank shoe store supermarket

1. Where does a teller work?

   A teller works at a _____.

2. Where does a salesperson work?

   A salesperson works at a _____.

3. Where does a cashier work?

   A cashier works at a _____.

D Look at the pictures. Write.

1. The customer is buying bandages at the _____.

2. The customer is buying _____.

3. _____.

25 The Supermarket

A Write.

celery	lettuce	tomato	avocado	apple
pineapple	orange	lemon	paper towels	box

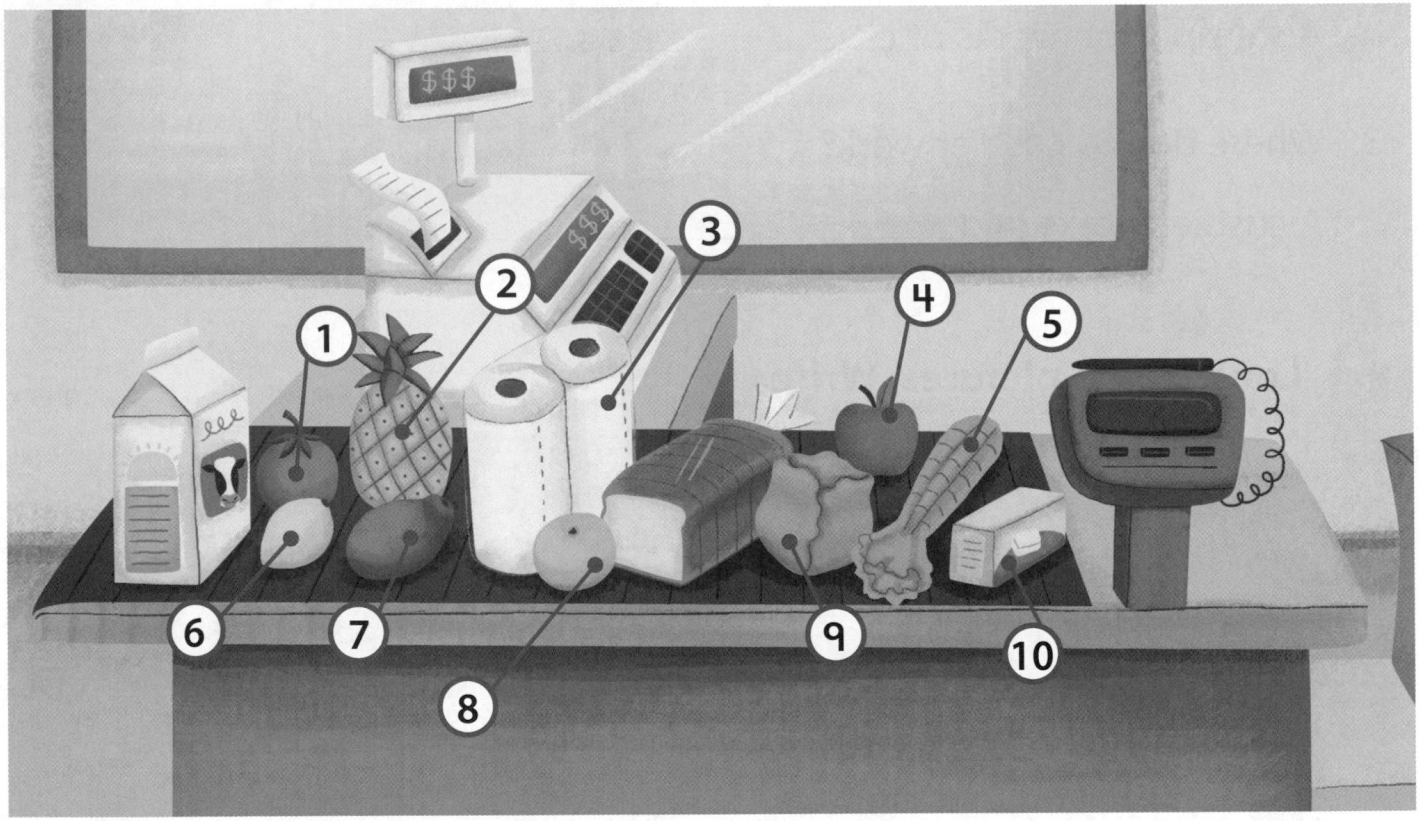

Grocery List

1. _____
2. _____
3. _____
4. _____
5. _____
6. _____
7. _____
8. _____
9. _____
10. _____ of butter

B Write.

1. She's going to buy an _____.

2. He's going to buy a _____.

3. They're going to buy a _____.

C Look at the picture. Write.

1. He's going to buy a carton of _____.

2. She's _____.

3. He's _____.

26 The Restaurant

A Circle the correct word.

1. 

soup rice

2. 

broccoli chicken

3. 

chicken rice

4. 

broccoli soup

5. 

fork spoon

6. 

knife napkin

B Write.

soup server order

1. Hello. I'm your _____.

2. Can I take your _____?

3. I'd like a bowl of _____, please.

C Write.

forks knife menu

1. She needs a _____.

2. He needs a _____.

3. They need _____.

D Look at the picture. Write.

1. He needs a _____.
2. He needs a _____ and a _____.
3. She _____.

27 The City

A Label.

helmet building bus stop bicycle seatbelt garden

1.  _____

2.  _____

3.  _____

4. 

_____

5.  _____

6.  _____

B Write.

Wait Ride Walk

1. _____ to the bus stop.

2. _____ for the bus.

3. _____ the bus.

C Write.

rides walks drives

1. Sammi _____.
2. Greg _____ a bicycle.
3. Mr. Jones _____ a car.

D Look at the picture. Write.

1. She drives a _____.
2. He _____.
3. She _____.

28 Transportation

A Match.

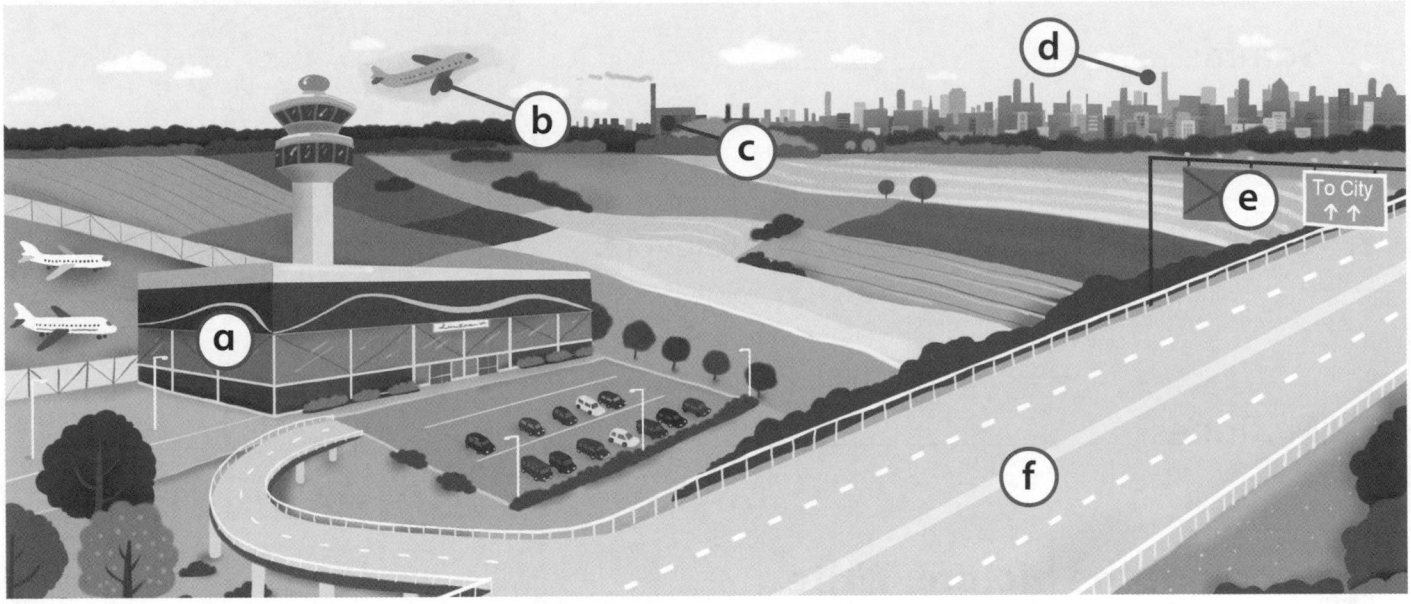

1. ___ airport
2. ___ factory
3. ___ sign
4. ___ skyscraper
5. ___ highway
6. ___ airplane

B Match.

airplane • police car • van • truck • motorcycle • train • helicopter •

• • • • • • •

C Look at A. Write *near* or *far*.

1. The factory is _____ from the airport.

2. The skyscrapers are _____ from the airport.

3. The airport is _____ the highway.

D Look at the picture. Write.

1. The van is _____ the airplane.

2. The truck is _____ the airport and

   _____ the city.

3. The motorcycle _____.

29 The Harbor

A Write.

sailboat	crane	tugboat	ferry	dock
lighthouse	ship	life jacket	bridge	

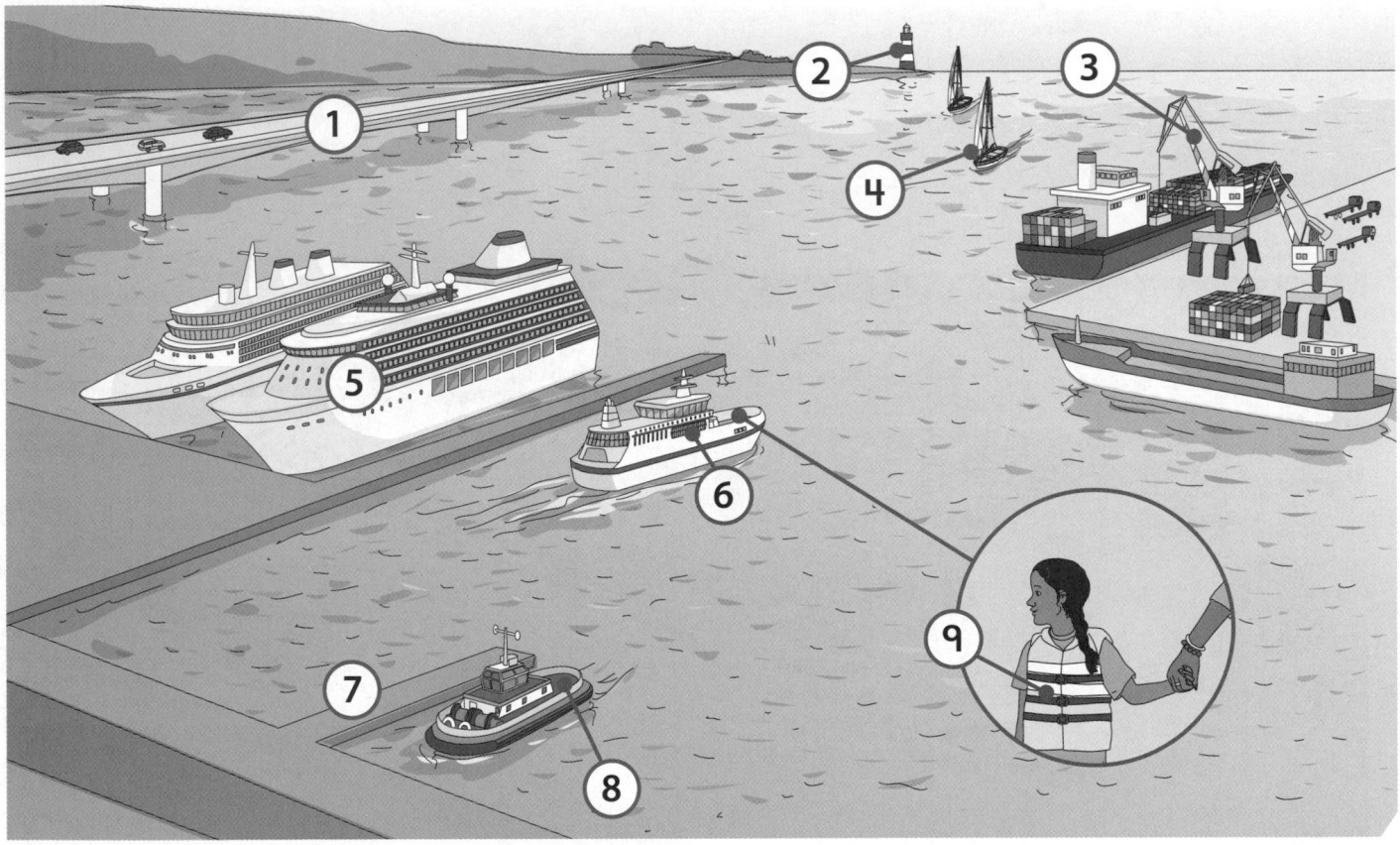

1. _____
2. _____
3. _____
4. _____
5. _____
6. _____
7. _____
8. _____
9. _____

B Look at A. Write.

1. How many lighthouses are on the harbor?

   One _____ is on the harbor.

2. How many _____ are on the bridge?

   Three _____ are on the _____.

3. How many _____ are in the harbor?

   Eight _____ are in the _____.

C Look at the picture. Write.

1. Ten people are on the _____.

2. Four people are _____.

3. Two _____.

30 The Hospital

A Match.

1. _____ cast
2. _____ X-ray
3. _____ wheelchair
4. _____ shot
5. _____ ambulance
6. _____ crutches

a.

b.

c.

d.

e.

f.

B Match.

1.

2.

3.

4.

5.

6.

surgeon

patient

receptionist

paramedic

doctor

baby

C Write.

1. Who is in the ambulance?

   The _____ is in the ambulance.

2. Who is in the emergency room?

   The _____ is in the emergency room.

3. Who is in the wheelchair?

   The _____ is in the wheelchair.

D Look at the pictures. Write.

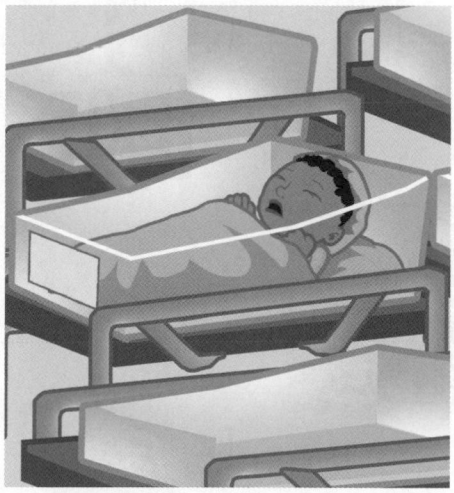

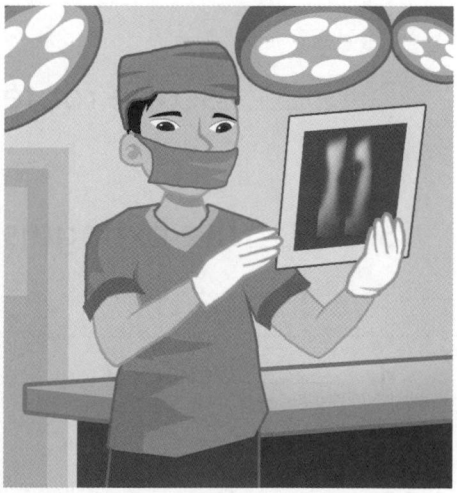

1. The _____ is in the nursery.

2. The _____ the emergency room.

3. _____.

31 Fire Safety

A Match.

1. _____ firefighter
2. _____ smoke
3. _____ fire truck
4. _____ matches
5. _____ uniform
6. _____ smoke detector
7. _____ escape route
8. _____ fire extinguisher
9. _____ battery
10. _____ fire escape
11. _____ exit
12. _____ call 911

a.

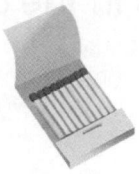

b.

c.

d.

e.

f.

g.

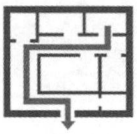

h.

i.

j.

k.

l.

B Write.

smoke detector 911 matches

1. Don't play with _____.

2. Make sure the _____ has a battery.

3. Call _____ for help.

C Look at the pictures. Write.

1. Know the _____.
2. Plan an _____.
3. Find the _____.

32 The Farm

A Circle the correct word.

1. farmer horse
2. tractor barn
3. cow chicken

4. horse cow
5. horse farmer
6. chicken tractor

B Label.

crop orchard field

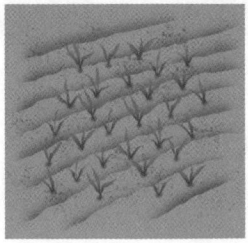

1. _____
2. _____
3. _____

C Write.

pick feeds plows

1. The farmer _____ the field.

2. She _____ the cow.

3. They _____ apples in the orchard.

D Look at the picture. Write.

1. She picks _____.

2. He plows _____.

3. They _____.

A Match.

1. 
2. 
3. 
4. 
5. 

bank

teller

cashier

hospital

mail carrier

police officer

police station

post office

receptionist

supermarket

6. 

7. 

8. 

9. 
10. 

B Look at the chart on page 80 of the *Dictionary*. Write.

1. A _____ works at a supermarket.
2. A police officer works at a _____.
3. A _____ works at a bank.
4. A _____ works at a post office.

C Complete the chart.

doctor	drugstore	farmer	farm	hospital
pharmacist	restaurant	salesperson	server	shoe store

People Who Work →	Places to Work

D Look at your chart in C. Write.

1. A server works at a _____.
2. A _____ works at a hospital.
3. A _____ works at a _____.
4. _____.
5. _____.

33 Biography Verbs

A Label.

trade	explore	invent	travel	sign a document
celebrate	be born	die	immigrate	

1. _____

2. _____

3. _____

4. _____

5. _____

6. _____

7. _____

8. _____

9. _____

B Write.

died signed born

1. George Washington was _____ in 1732.

2. He _____ the Constitution in 1787.

3. He _____ in 1799.

C Look at the pictures. Write.

1. Marco was _____ in _____.

2. He _____ to Washington, D.C. in _____.

3. He _____ his eighth birthday in _____.

34 Map Skills

A Match.

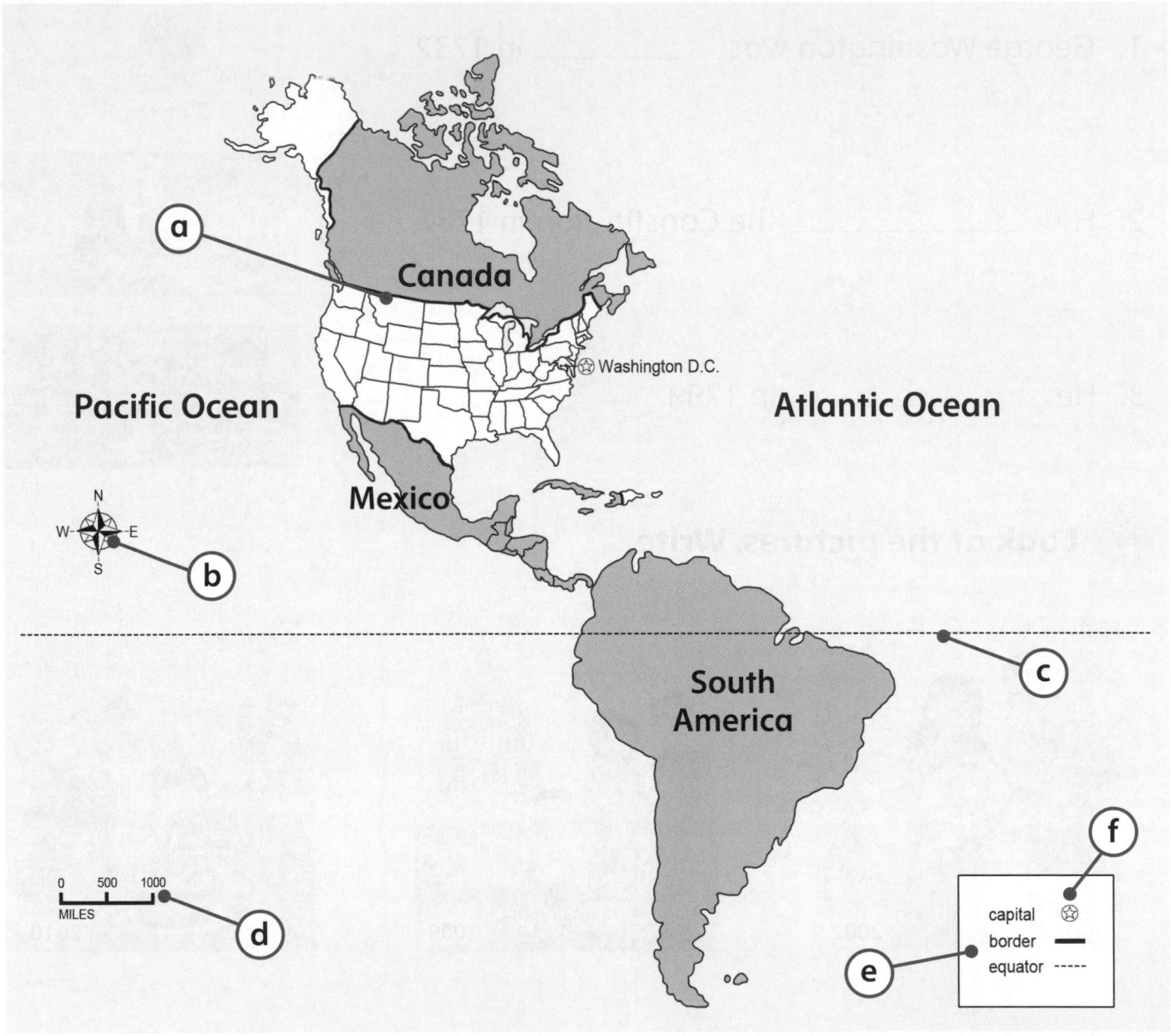

1. ____ compass rose
2. ____ border
3. ____ key
4. ____ scale
5. ____ equator
6. ____ symbol

B Write.

1. This is a _____.

2. This is a _____.

3. This is a _____.

C Look at the picture. Color the oceans blue. Color the continents green. Then write.

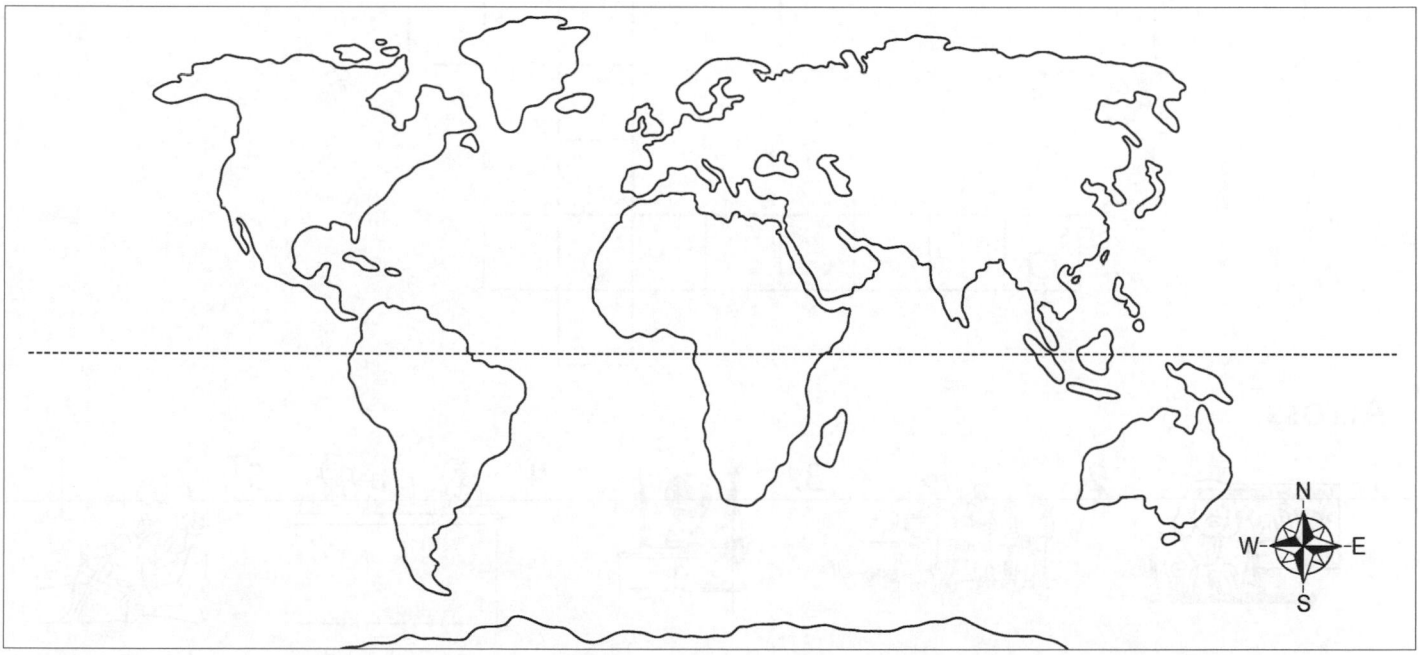

1. The map shows the oceans and _____.
2. The color blue shows _____.
3. The color green _____.

35 The Government

A Write.

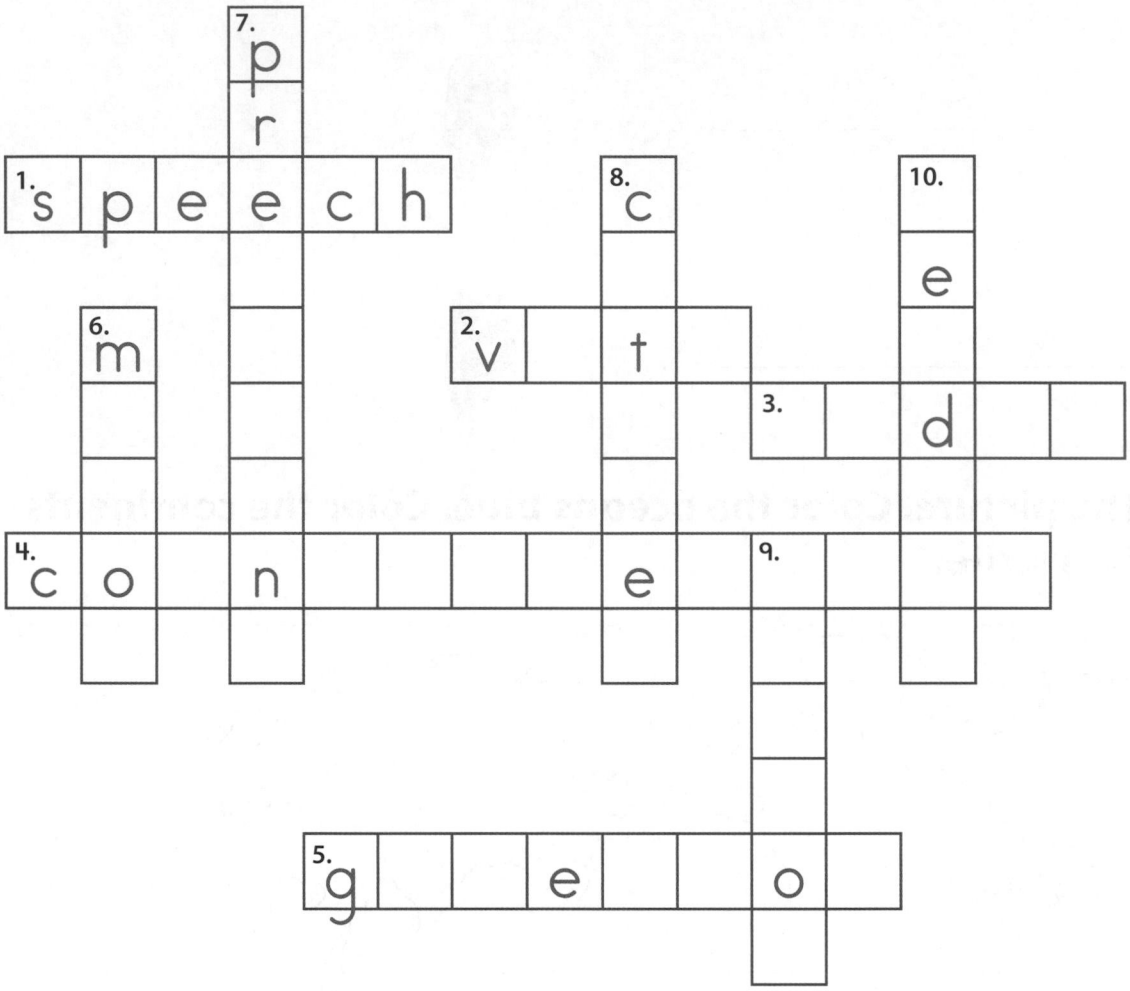

Across

1. 

2. 

3. 

4. 

5. 

Down

6. 

7. 

8. 

9. 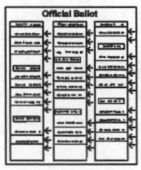

10. 

B Write.

president judge city council

1. Who leads the citizens?

   The _____ leads the citizens.

2. Who leads the country?

   The _____ leads the country.

3. Who leads the courtroom?

   The _____ leads the courtroom.

C Look at the pictures. Write.

1. The mayor leads the _____.

2. The governor _____.

3. _____.

36 American Symbols

A Label.

Capitol	Congress	Supreme Court	monument
memorial	stars	stripes	Pledge of Allegiance

1. 

_____

2. 

_____

3. 

_____

4. 

_____

5. 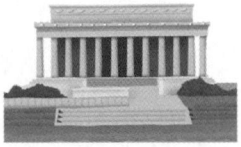

_____

6. 

_____

7. 

_____

8. 

_____

B Write.

national anthem	White House	eagle

1. What is the bald _____?

   It's a national symbol.

2. What is "The Star Spangled Banner"?

   It's the _____.

3. What is the _____?

   It's the home of the President.

C Look at the pictures. Write.

1. The Lincoln Memorial is a national _____.
2. The Statue of Liberty is a _____.
3. The Capitol is a _____.

A Match.

1. _____ monument

a.

b.

2. _____ Supreme Court

c.

3. _____ city council

4. _____ governor

d.

e.

5. _____ national anthem

B Look at the chart on page 90 in the *Dictionary*. Write.

1. The city has a _____ and a _____.
2. The state has a _____ and a _____.
3. The country has a _____, a _____, and a _____.

C Complete the chart.

The United States		country	state	city
Congress				
mayor				
citizens				
president				
memorial				

D Look at your chart in C. Write.

1. The country has a president, Congress, and _____.
2. The country doesn't have a _____.
3. The state has a _____ and _____.
4. The state doesn't have a _____.
5. _____.

37 Healthy Habits

A Match.

exercise ● sleep ● floss ● drink water ● wear sunblock ●

● ● ● ● ●

B Write.

Wash Cover Use

1. _____ your mouth.

2. _____ a tissue.

3. _____ your hands.

C Write.

goes to the dentist gets a checkup exercises

1. She _____ every day.

2. He _____ every six months.

3. She _____ every year.

D Look at the pictures. Write.

1. She _____ every day.

2. He _____.

3. She _____.

38 Faces

A Write.

cheek	eyebrow	tongue	chin	teeth	ear
mouth	lip	eyelid	gum	nose	forehead

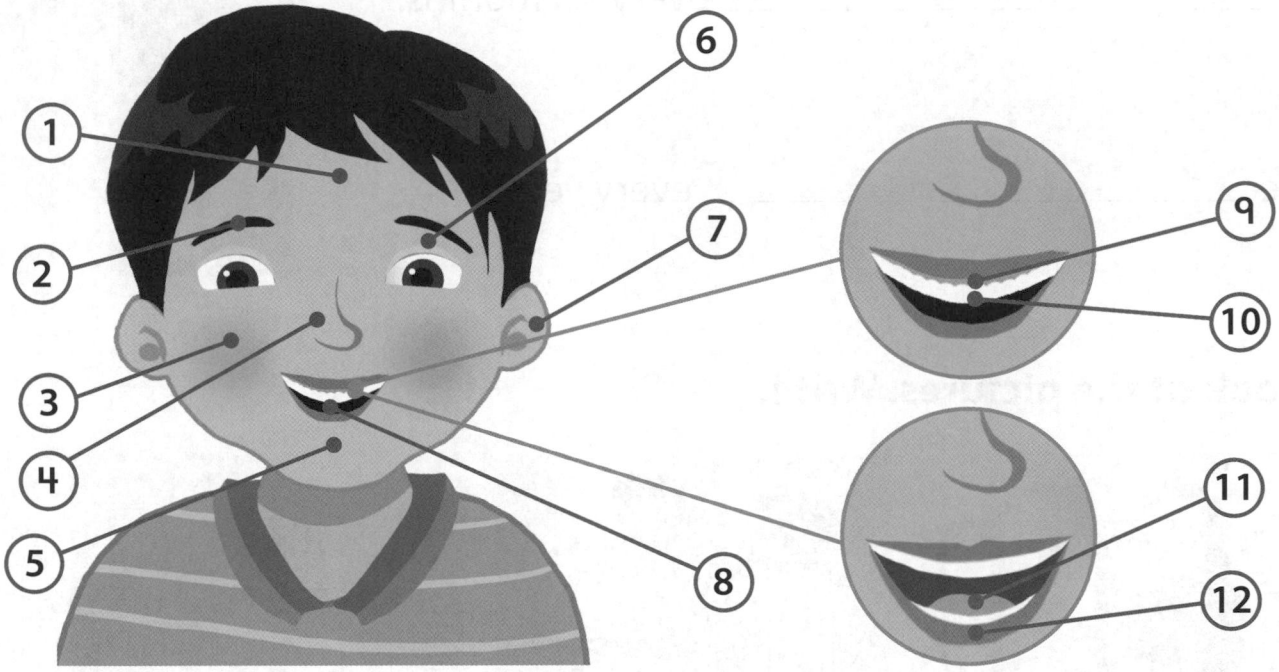

1. _____
2. _____
3. _____
4. _____
5. _____
6. _____
7. _____
8. _____
9. _____
10. _____
11. _____
12. _____

B Look at A. Write *above* or *below*.

1. His forehead is _____ his eyebrows.
2. His eyebrows are _____ his eyelids.
3. His cheeks are _____ his eyes.

C Look at the picture. Write.

1. Lucy's eyes and nose are _____.
2. Tasha's nose and _____.
3. Emma's lips and _____.

39 Parts of the Body

A Write the missing vowels: *a, e, i, o,* or *u*.

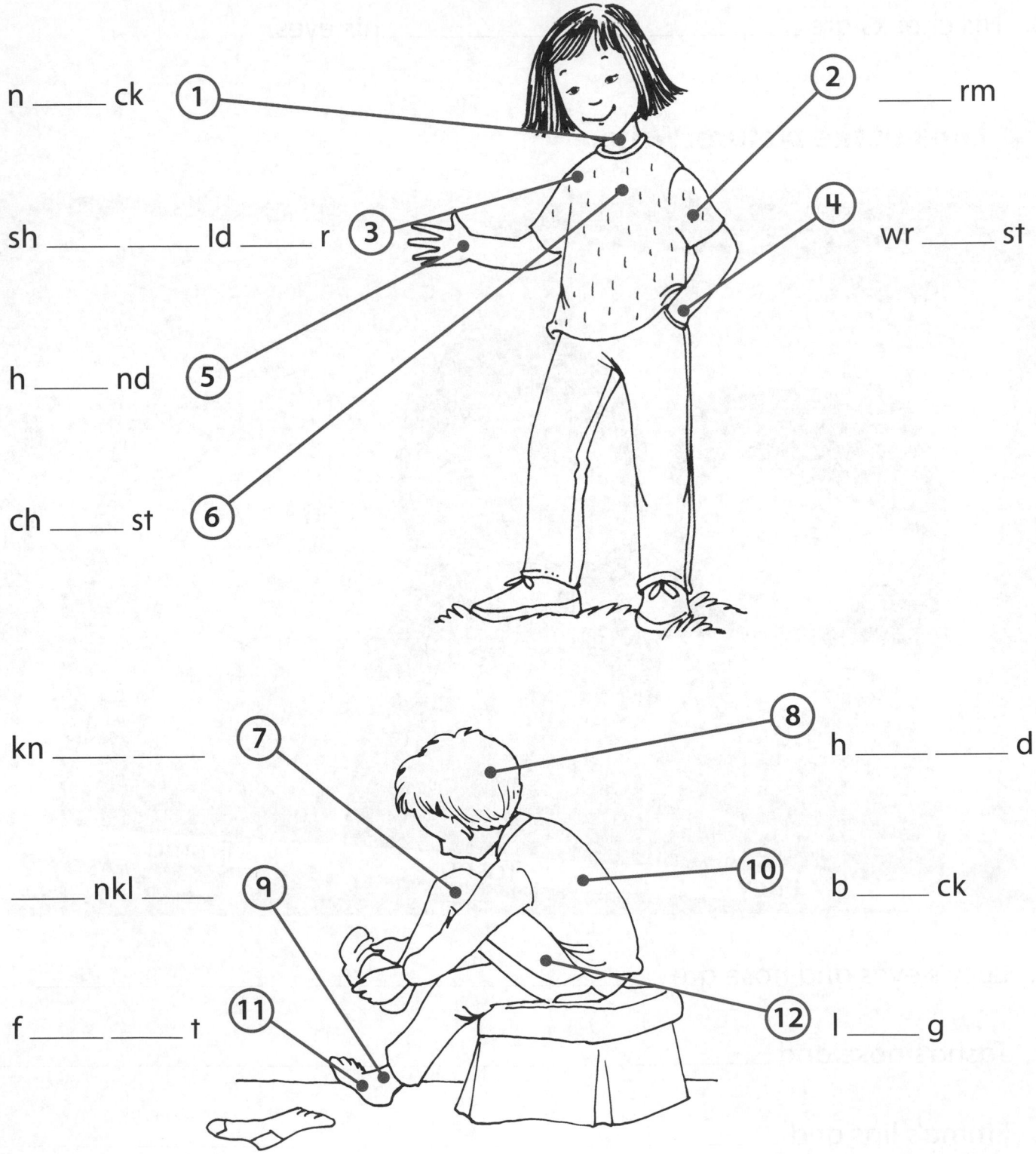

B Write.

shoulders foot head hand leg arm

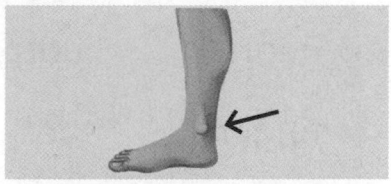

1. The ankle is between the _____ and the _____.

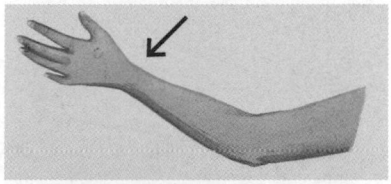

2. The wrist is between the _____ and the _____.

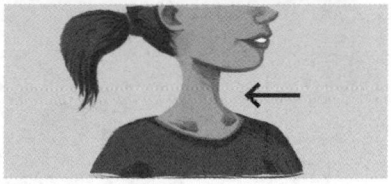

3. The neck is between the _____ and the _____.

C Look at the picture. Write.

1. The chest is between the _____ and the arms.
2. The ankle _____.
3. The wrist _____.

40 More Parts of the Body

A Write.

heart	lung	brain	stomach	muscle
finger	toe	bone	rib	

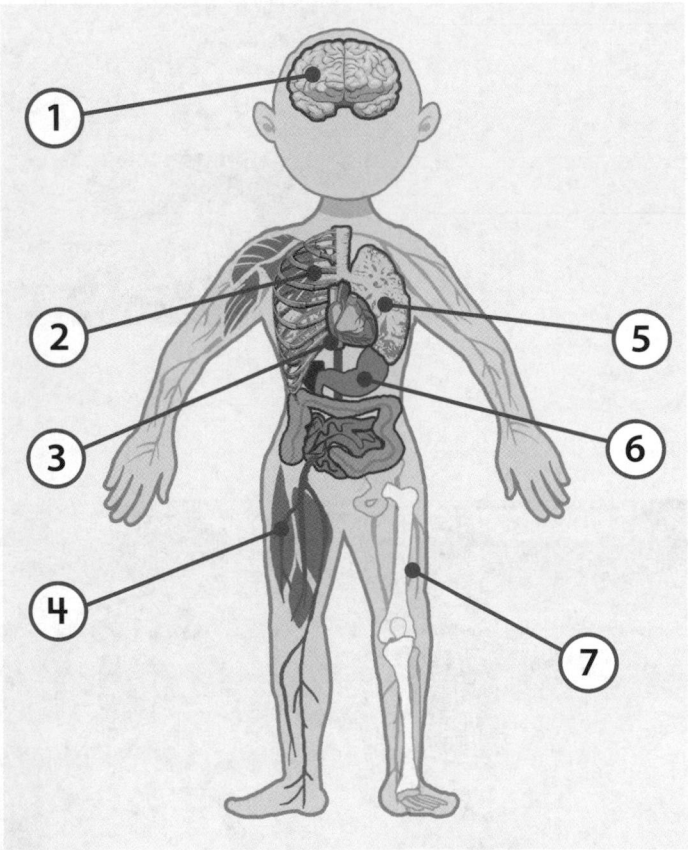

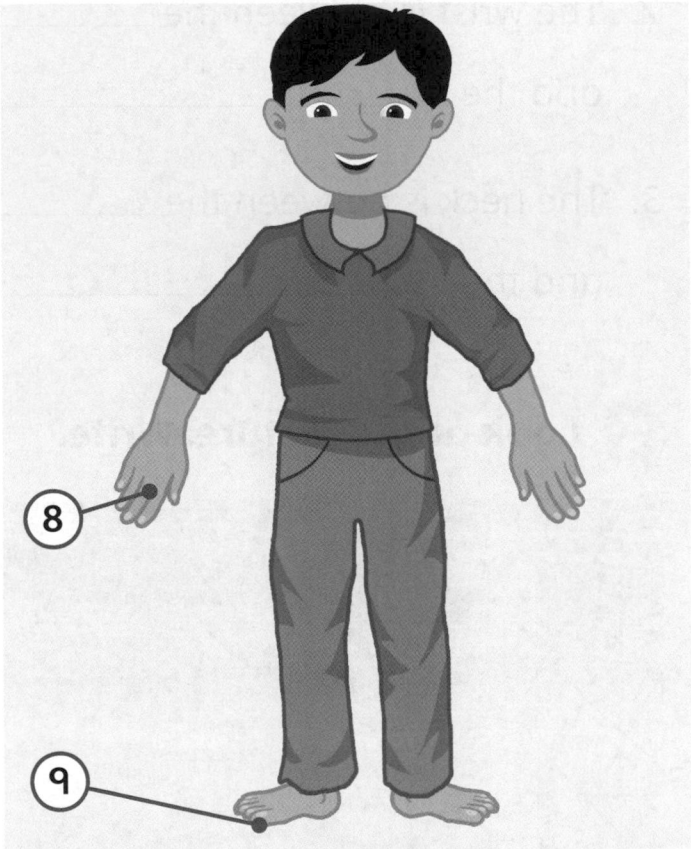

1. _____
2. _____
3. _____
4. _____
5. _____
6. _____
7. _____
8. _____
9. _____

B Write.

1. The _____ is in the head.

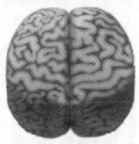

2. The _____ is in the chest.

3. The _____ is on the body.

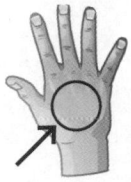

C Look at the picture. Write.

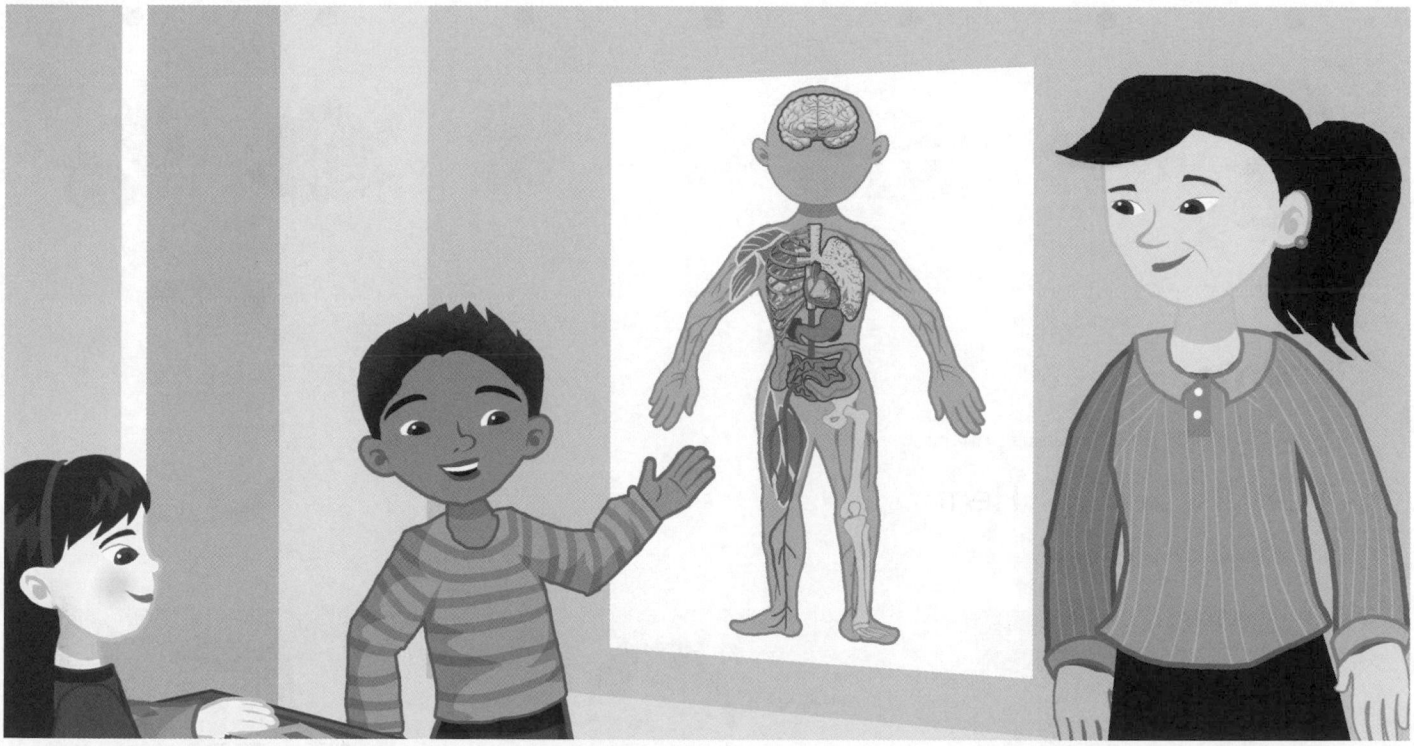

1. The lungs and heart are in the _____.
2. The brain is _____.
3. The muscles and bones _____.

41 The Senses

A Match.

shiny • rough • smooth • sweet • sour • loud • quiet •

B Write.

Feel See Hear

1. _____
the shiny airplane.

2. _____
the loud music.

3. _____
the smooth stone.

C Write.

sees tastes smells

1. He _____ the sour lemon.

2. She _____ the sweet flower.

3. He _____ the shiny star.

D Look at the picture. Write.

1. He hears the _____ triangle.

2. He feels the _____.

3. He _____.

42 Nutrition

A Match.

1. _____ nuts
2. _____ peach
3. _____ corn
4. _____ pear
5. _____ oatmeal
6. _____ peppers
7. _____ pasta
8. _____ fish
9. _____ cheese
10. _____ sweet potato
11. _____ yogurt
12. _____ spinach

a.

b.

c.

d.

e.

f.

g.

h.

i.

j.

k.

l.

B Write.

1. _____ are part of the meat and bean group.

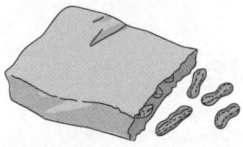

2. _____ and _____ are part of the milk group.

3. _____ and _____ are part of the vegetable group.

C Look at the picture. Write.

1. Sweet potatoes and spinach are part of the _____.
2. Peaches and _____.
3. Bread _____.

A Label.

bone	heart	lips	lungs	neck
toe	head	eyebrow	fingernail	

1. 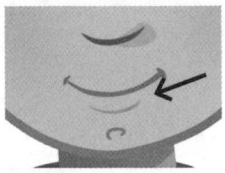 _____

2.  _____

3. 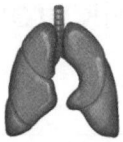 _____

4. 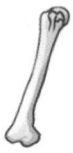 _____

5. 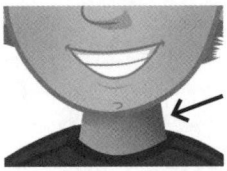 _____

6. 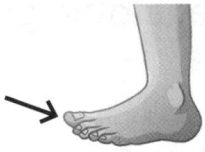 _____

7. 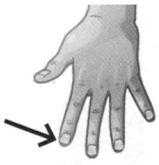 _____

8.  _____

9.  _____

B Look at the chart on page 104 of the *Dictionary*. Write.

1. I have many toes, _____, and _____.
2. I have two eyebrows, _____,
   and _____.
3. I have one head, _____, and _____.

C Complete the chart.

back	brain	ears	knees	muscles
shoulders	stomach	teeth	toenails	

Parts of the Body		
one	**two**	**many**

D Look at your chart in C. Write.

1. I have _____ stomach.
2. I have _____ knees.
3. I have _____ teeth and muscles.
4. I don't have two _____.
5. I don't have _____.
6. _____.

43 Observe and Measure

A Label.

ruler	magnifying glass	measure	thermometer	binoculars
observe	measuring cup	microscope	measuring tape	meter stick

1.  _____

2. 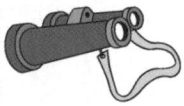 _____

3.  _____

4.  _____

5.  _____

6.  _____

7. 

_____

8.  _____

9.  _____

10.  _____

B Write *measure* or *observe*.

1. Use a microscope to _____.
2. Use a thermometer to _____.
3. Use binoculars to _____.

C Look at the picture. Write.

1. Use a measuring tape to _____.
2. Use a _____ to observe.
3. Use a _____.

44 Plants

A Write.

thorn	petal	bulb	pollen	bee	flower
seed	seedling	stem	roots	bud	leaf

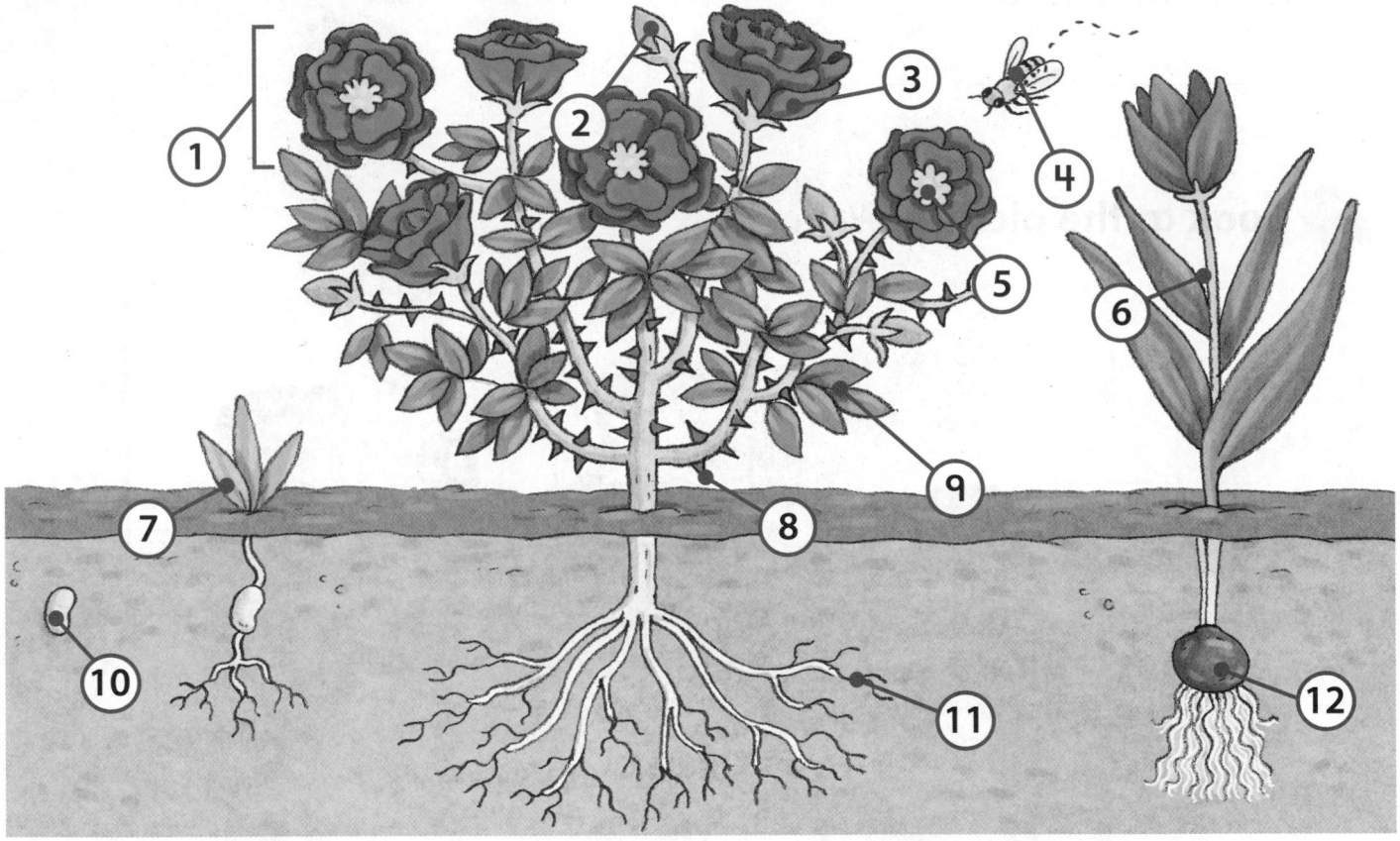

1. _____
2. _____
3. _____
4. _____
5. _____
6. _____
7. _____
8. _____
9. _____
10. _____
11. _____
12. _____

B Write *large* or *small*.

1. The beans have _____ seeds.

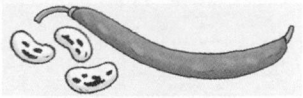

2. The seedling has _____ leaves.

3. The rose has _____ thorns.

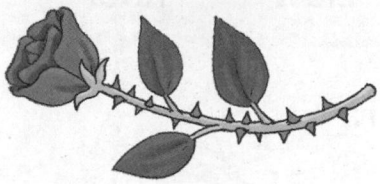

C Look at the picture. Write.

1. Sunflowers have large flowers and _____ seeds.

2. Tulips have _____ leaves and

   _____ petals.

3. Roses _____.

45 Animals in the Zoo

A Label.

tail	beak	wing	feather	paw	fur
claw	hoof	antlers	pouch	whiskers	shell

1. 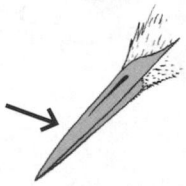 _____

2.  _____

3.  _____

4.  _____

5.  _____

6.  _____

7.  _____

8.  _____

9.  _____

10.  _____

11. 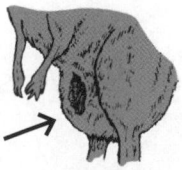 _____

12. 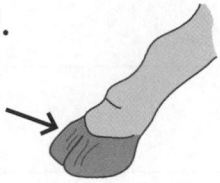 _____

B Write.

1. Which animal has fur?

   The _____ has fur.

2. Which animal has feathers?

   The _____ has feathers.

3. Which animals have tails?

   The _____ and the _____ have tails.

C Look at the picture. Write.

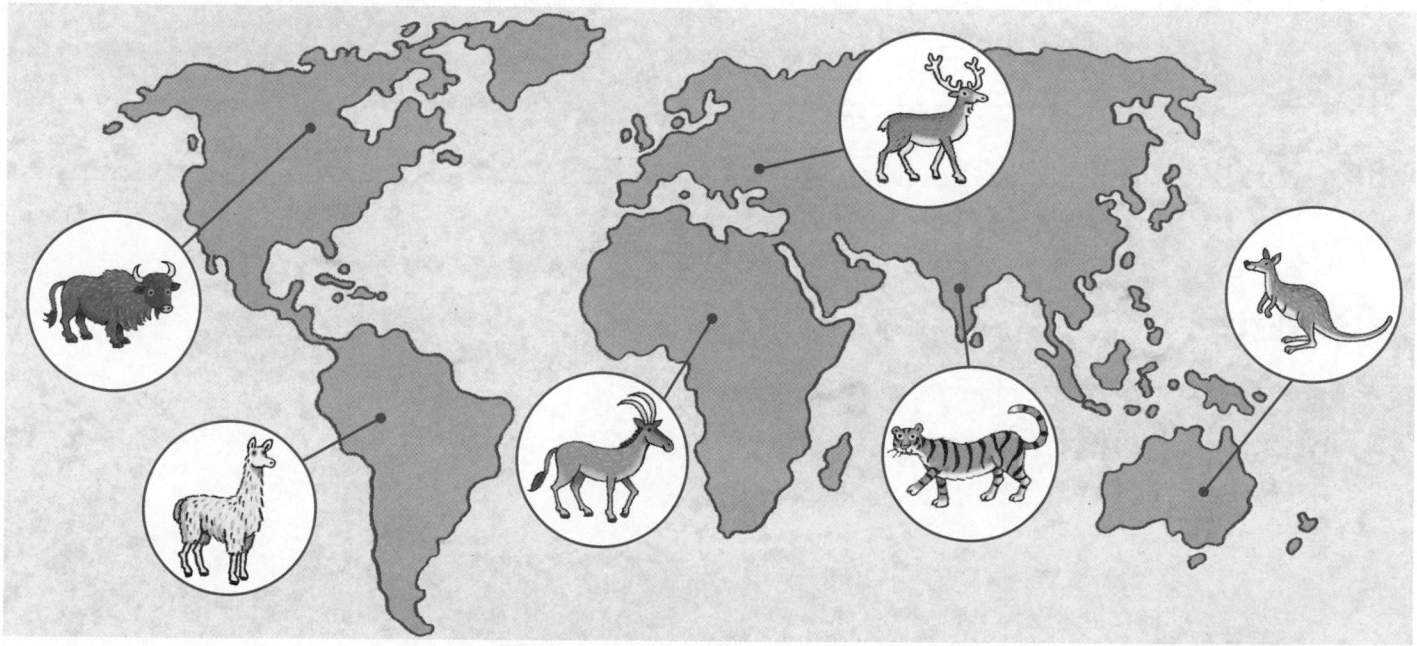

1. The kangaroo has a _____ and a _____.

2. The antelope has _____ and _____.

3. The tiger, the antelope, and the kangaroo have _____.

46 Growing and Changing

A Write.

cocoon egg caterpillar butterfly

1. _____ 2. _____

3. _____ 4. _____

B Write.

hatch chick egg nest

1.  _____

2.  _____

3. 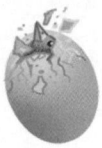 _____

4.  _____

C Write.

cat tadpole bird kitten frog chick

1. The _____

   becomes a _____.

2. The _____

   becomes a _____.

3. The _____

   becomes a _____.

D Look at the picture. Write.

1. The chicks become _____.

2. The caterpillar becomes a _____.

3. _____.

47 The Ocean

A Write the words in the puzzle.

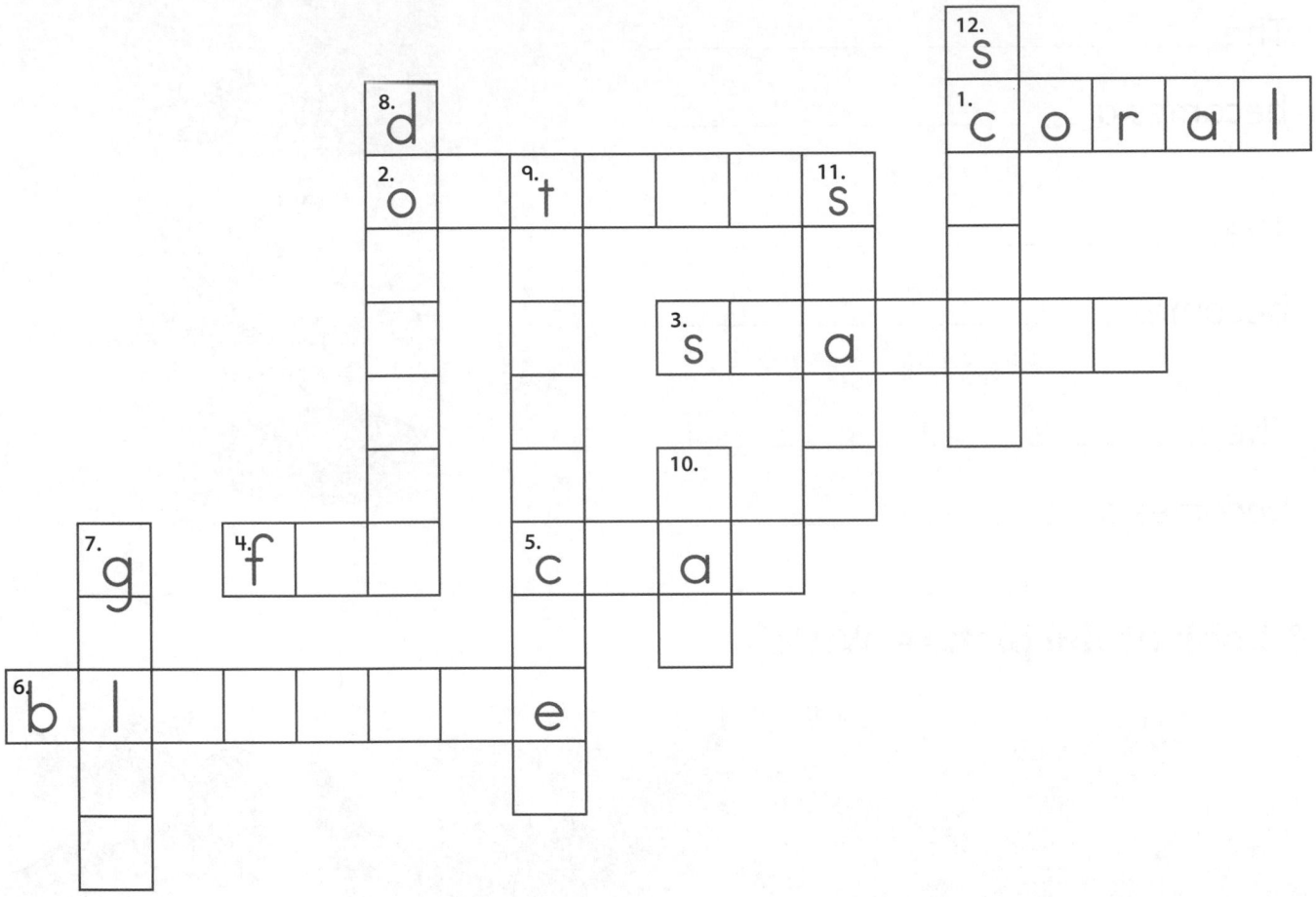

Across

1. 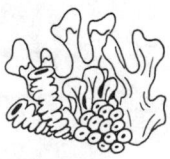
2. 
3. 
4. 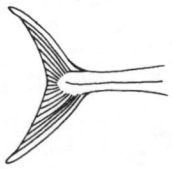
5. 
6. 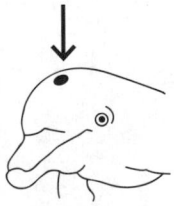

Down

7. 
8. 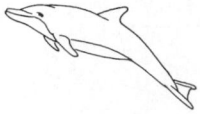
9. 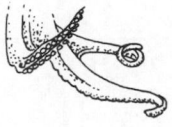
10. 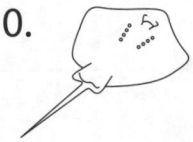
11. 
12. 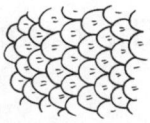

B Write.

1. A _____

   has _____.

2. An _____

   has _____.

3. A _____

   has a _____.

C Look at the picture. Write.

1. A crab has claws and a _____.

2. An octopus has eight _____ and

   a crab has eight _____.

3. A shark and a ray have _____.

48 The Desert

A Match.

1. _____ coyote
2. _____ hawk
3. _____ lizard
4. _____ mouse
5. _____ prairie dog
6. _____ rabbit
7. _____ scorpion
8. _____ snake

a.

b.

c.

d.

e.

f.

g.

h.

B Write.

dunes hole cactus sand

1. 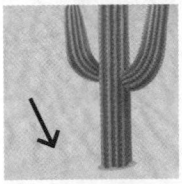 _____

2.  _____

3. 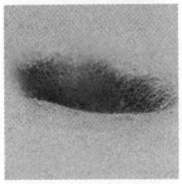 _____

4.  _____

C Write.

1. The _____ hides under the rock.

2. The _____ hides in the hole.

3. The _____ hides in the _____.

D Look at the picture. Write.

1. The bird hides in the _____.
2. The lizard _____.
3. _____.

49 The Forest

A Match.

1. _____ oak tree
2. _____ needles
3. _____ acorns
4. _____ pine tree
5. _____ pine cone

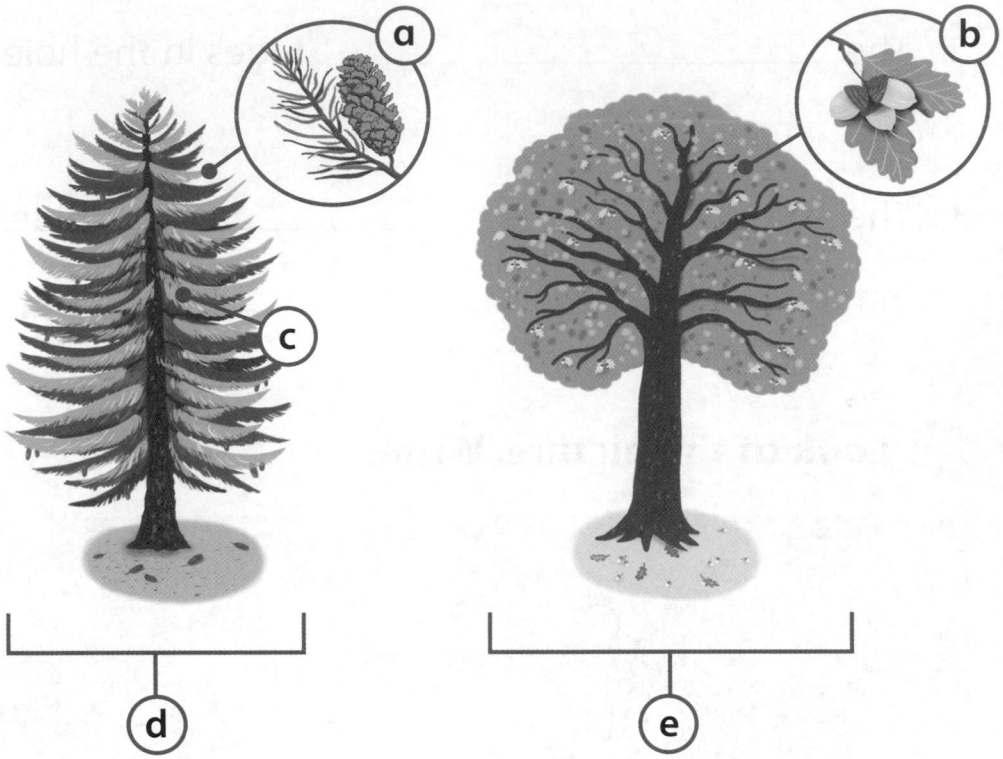

B Write.

deer mosquito squirrel woodpecker bear

1. 

_____

2. 

_____

3. 

_____

4. 

_____

5. 

_____

C Write.

1. A pine tree has a _____.

   An oak tree has a _____ too.

2. An oak tree has _____.

   A pine tree has _____ too.

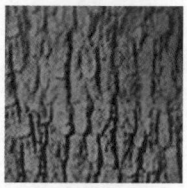

3. A bear has _____.

   A deer has _____ too.

D Look at the picture. Write.

1. An oak tree and a pine tree have _____.

2. A hawk and a woodpecker _____.

3. A rabbit and _____.

50 The Rain Forest

A Match.

1. 

2. 

3. 

4. 

moth

turtle

parrot

owl

dragonfly

spider

bat

jaguar

5. 

6. 

7. 

8. 

B Write.

moss fern orchid

1. 

_____

2. 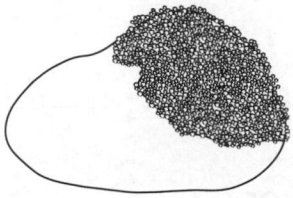

_____

3. 

_____

C Write *flies* or *walks*.

1. A bat _____.

2. An owl _____.

3. An ant _____.

D Look at the picture. Write.

1. An ant and a spider _____.

2. A _____ and a _____ fly.

3. A jaguar and _____.

51 The Grassland

A Write.

elephant	hyena	lion	flamingo
hippopotamus	giraffe	zebra	leopard

1. 

_____

2. 

_____

3. 

_____

4. 

_____

5. 

_____

6. 

_____

7. 

_____

8. 

_____

B Write *spots* or *stripes*.

1. A leopard has _____.

2. A zebra has _____.

3. A giraffe has _____.

C Look at the picture. Write.

1. The elephants are near the _____.

2. The zebras are far from _____.

3. The lion _____.

A Label.

fin tail paw wing

1. 

_____

2. 

_____

3. 

_____

4. 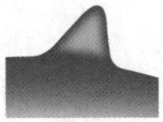

_____

B Look at the chart on page 124 of the *Dictionary*. Write.

1. A _____ has a tail and fins.
2. A _____ has a tail and wings.
3. A _____ and a _____ have a tail and paws.
4. A fish, squirrel, lion, _____, and _____ have a tail.

C Complete the chart.

Animal Features			
	feathers	scales	fur
fish			
snake			
squirrel			
parrot			
lion			

D Look at your chart in C. Write.

1. A parrot has _____.
2. A parrot does not have _____ or _____.
3. A squirrel and a lion have _____.
4. A squirrel and a lion do not have _____.
5. _____.

52 Experiment and Record

A Match.

1. _____ predict
2. _____ test
3. _____ pour
4. _____ record
5. _____ compare
6. _____ sort
7. _____ explain

a.

b.

c.

d.

e.

f.

g.

B Write.

graph diagram chart

1.

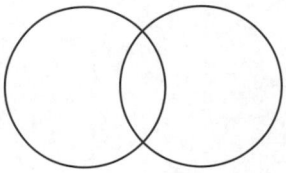

_____

2.

Student	Height	Weight
Ken	59"	96 lbs
Anna	58"	85 lbs
Louis	64"	120 lbs
Zennie	61"	109 lbs

_____

3.

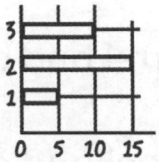

_____

C Write.

1. First, _____.

   Then, _____ it.

2. First, _____.

   Then, _____ a diagram.

3. First, make a _____.

   Then, _____ it.

D Look at the pictures. Write.

1. _____, predict. _____, test it.

2. First, _____ the milk and the water.

   Then, _____ the weights.

3. _____.

53 Matter

A Match.

1. 
2. 
3. 

ice

gas

wood

metal

liquid

solid

4. 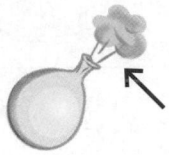
5. 
6. 

B Write.

freeze mix boil float sink melt

1. 

_____

2. 

_____

3. 

_____

4. 

_____

5. 

_____

6. 

_____

C Write *float, sink,* or *melt.*

1. Does metal _____?

   Yes, metal _____s.

2. Does wood _____?

   Yes, wood _____s.

3. Does ice _____?

   Yes, ice _____s.

D Look at the pictures. Write.

1. She _____ the water to make _____ cubes.

2. She _____ the _____ to make tea.

3. He _____ the _____,

   _____, and lemon to make iced tea.

54 Heat, Light, and Sound

A Write the words in the puzzle.

Across

1. 
2. 
3. 
4. 
5. 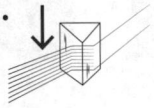
6. 
7. 

Down

8. 
9. 
10. 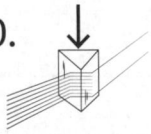
11. 
12. 

B Write.

light sound heat

1. The piano is a source of _____.
2. The rainbow is a source of _____.
3. The iron is a source of _____.

C Look at the picture. Write.

1. The grill is a source of _____.
2. The fire is a source of _____ and _____.
3. The drum and guitar are _____.

55 Motion and Force

A Match.

1. _____ push
2. _____ stop
3. _____ pull
4. _____ speed up
5. _____ slow down
6. _____ drop
7. _____ roll
8. _____ attract

a.

b.

c.

d.

e.

f.

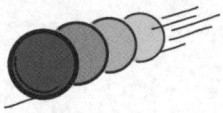

g.

h.

B Write.

slide swing wheel magnet

1.

_____

2.

_____

3.

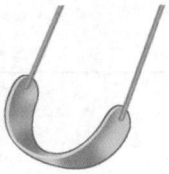

_____

4.

_____

C Write.

1. The ball is _____ing.

2. It's _____ing up.

3. Now it's _____ing down and stopping.

D Look at the picture. Write.

1. Jimmy's mother is _____ the ball.
2. Sally's father is _____.
3. Mike's big sister _____.

56 Energy and Electricity

A Label.

cord	plug	outlet	flashlight
light switch	light bulb	lawn mower	wire

1. 

_____

2. 

_____

3. 

_____

4. 

_____

5. 

_____

6. 

_____

7. 

_____

8. 

_____

B Write.

batteries electricity gas fan

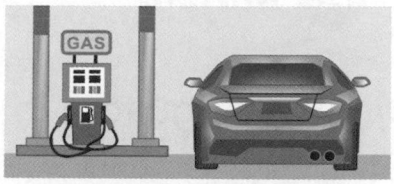

1. The car runs on _____.

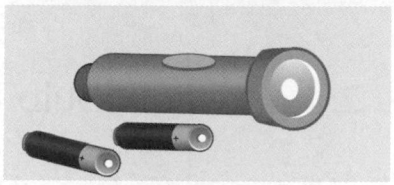

2. The flashlight runs on _____.

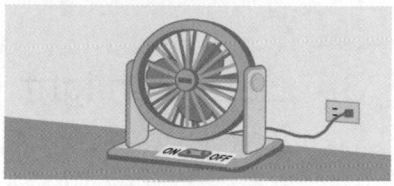

3. The _____ runs on _____.

C Look at the picture. Write.

1. The light bulb runs on _____.
2. The toy car _____.
3. The lawn mower _____.

A Match.

1. _____ guitar
2. _____ light bulb
3. _____ flashlight
4. _____ candle
5. _____ iron

a.

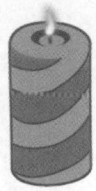

b.

c.

d.

e.

B Look at the chart on page 136 of the *Dictionary*. Write *heat, light,* or *sound.*

1. A guitar is a source of _____.
2. A light bulb is a source of _____.
3. An iron is a source of _____.
4. A flashlight is a source of _____.
5. A candle is a source of _____ and _____.

C Complete the chart.

Electricity		
	uses electricity	doesn't use electricity
light bulb		
guitar		
iron		
candle		
flashlight		

D Look at your chart in C. Write.

1. A light bulb uses _____.
2. A _____ doesn't use electricity.
3. An iron _____.
4. _____.
5. _____.

57 Land and Water

A Match.

1. _____ volcano
2. _____ island
3. _____ plain
4. _____ canyon
5. _____ plateau
6. _____ peninsula
7. _____ mountain

a.
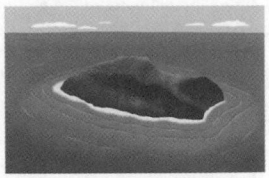

b.

c.

d.

e.
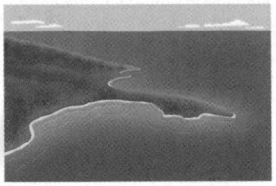

f.

g.

B Label.

lake gulf bay

1.
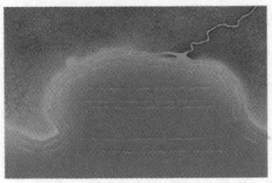

_____

2.

_____

3.
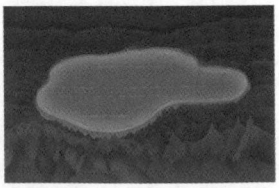

_____

C Write.

1. Is a lake a landform or a body of water?

   It's a _____.

2. Is a bay a landform or a body of water?

   It's a _____.

3. Is a volcano a landform or a body of water?

   It's a _____.

D Look at the picture. Write.

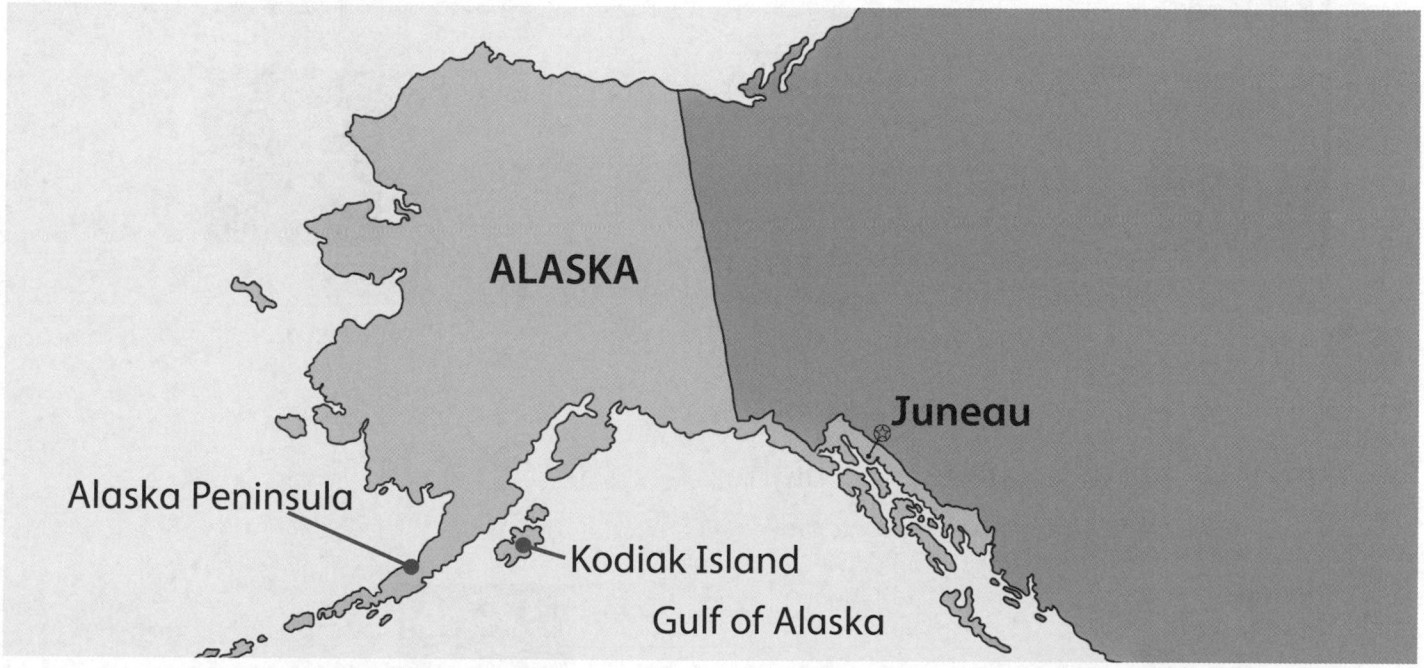

1. Kodiak Island is a _____.

2. The Gulf of Alaska _____.

3. The Alaska Peninsula _____.

58 In the Mountains

A Match.

1. 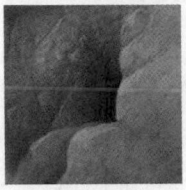
2. 
3. 
4. 

mountain range

dam

glacier

waterfall

cliff

cave

valley

hill

5. 
6. 
7. 
8. 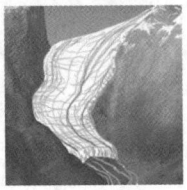

B Write

steep low level high

1. 

_____

2. 

_____

3. 

_____

4. 

_____

C Write.

low level high

1. The valley is _____.
2. The plateau is _____.
3. The mountain range is _____.

D Look at the picture. Write.

1. The glacier is _____.
2. The _____ is high.
3. _____.

59 Earth Materials

A Label.

crystal	pebble	mud	layer	soil
clay	rocks	lava	boulder	models

1.  _____

2.  _____

3.  _____

4. 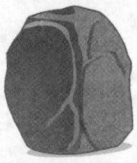 _____

5.  _____

6. 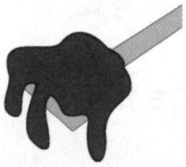 _____

7.  _____

8.  _____

9.  _____

10.  _____

B Write *hard* or *soft*.

1. The clay is _____.
2. The boulder is _____.
3. The mud is _____.

C Look at the picture. Write.

1. The pebble is _____.
2. The soil _____.
3. _____.

60 Dinosaurs and Fossils

A Match.

1. _____ skull
2. _____ skeleton
3. _____ horn
4. _____ spike
5. _____ footprint
6. _____ fossil
7. _____ dinosaur
8. _____ scientist

B Write *meat-eater* or *plant-eater*.

1.

_____

2.

_____

3.

_____

C Write.

sharp spikes flat

1. Plant-eaters had _____ teeth.

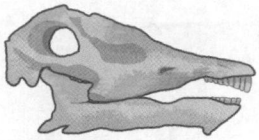

2. Meat-eaters had _____ teeth.

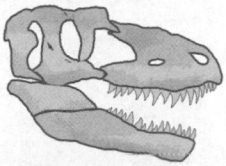

3. Stegosaurus had _____.

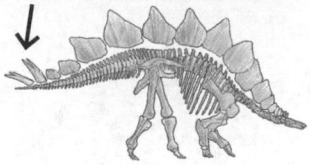

D Look at the picture. Write.

1. Tyrannosaurus rex had _____ teeth.

2. Triceratops had _____.

3. Stegosaurus _____.

61 Weather

A Circle the correct word.

1. 
   fog
   wind

2. 
   sunshine
   snow

3. 
   blizzard
   sunshine

4. 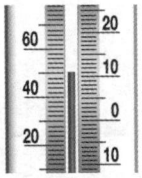

   temperature
   wind

5. 
   tornado
   temperature

6. 
   rain
   snow

7. 
   tornado
   hail

8. 
   fog
   hail

B Write.

hurricane rain thunderstorm lightning

1. 
   _____

2. 
   _____

3. 
   _____

4. 
   _____

C Write about yesterday's weather.

1. There was a _____ in New York.
2. There was a _____ in Oklahoma City.
3. There was a _____ in Los Angeles.

D Look at the picture. Write.

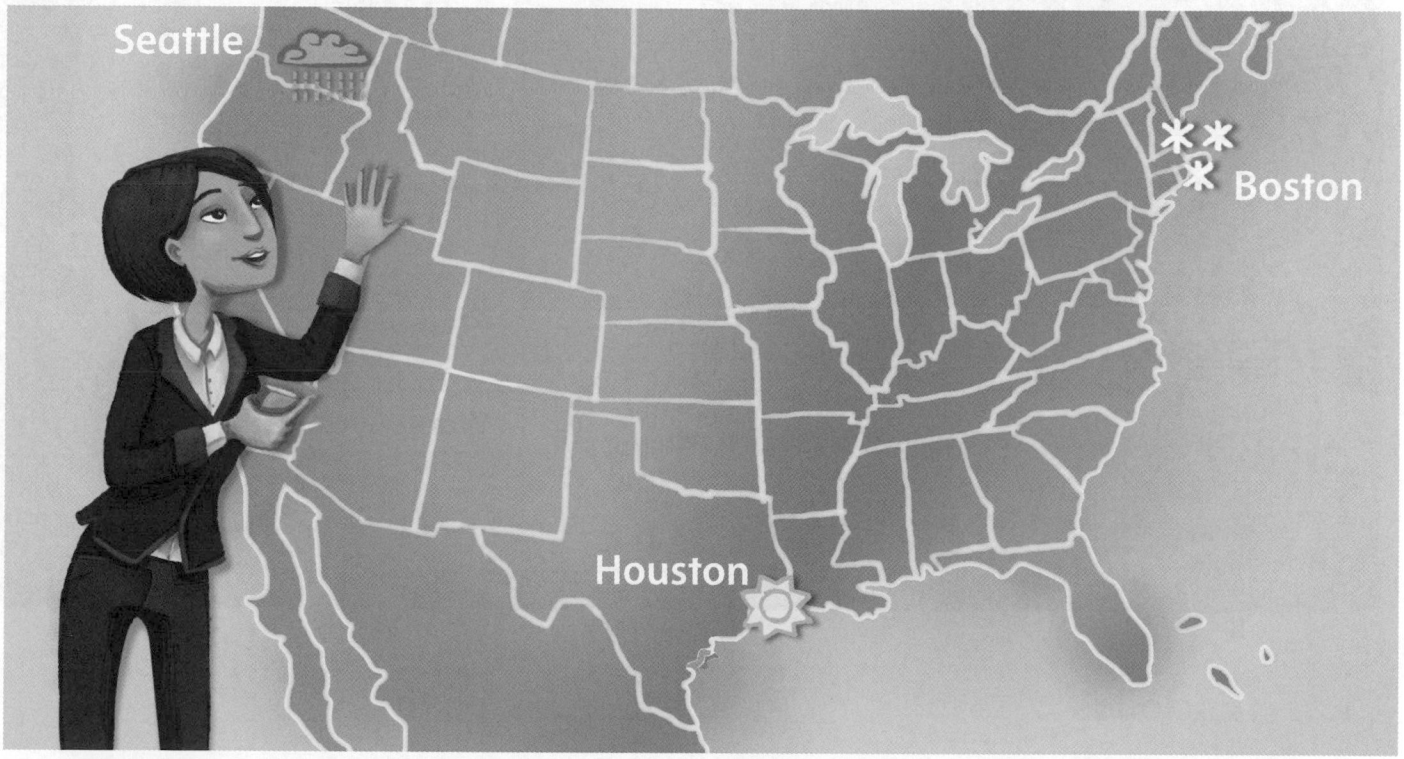

1. There was _____ in Seattle.
2. There was _____.
3. _____.

62 On the Coast

A Match.

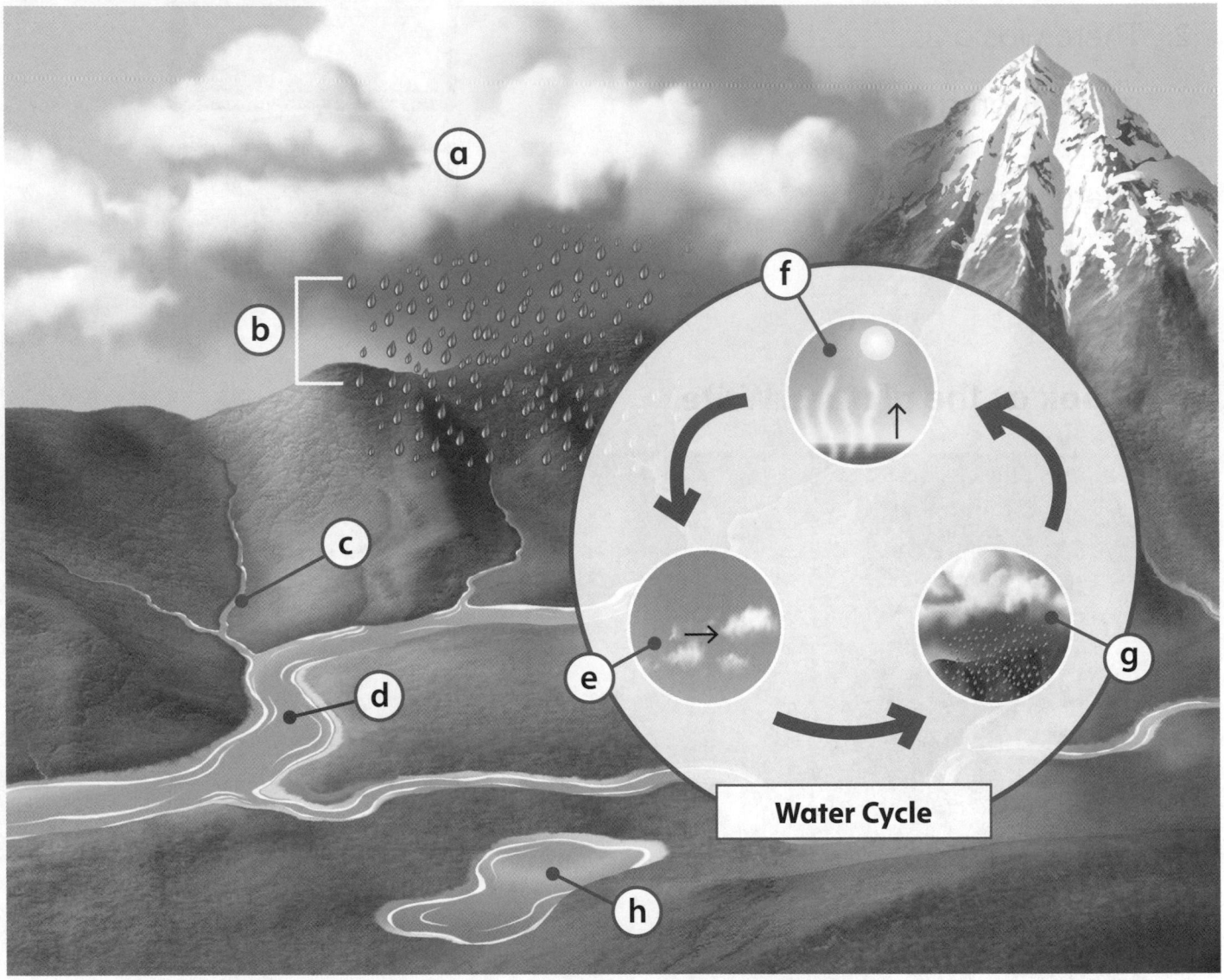

1. _____ clouds
2. _____ condensation
3. _____ drops
4. _____ evaporation
5. _____ pond
6. _____ precipitation
7. _____ river
8. _____ stream

B Write.

Precipitation	stream	ocean	lake	sea	Condensation

1. A _____ has fresh water.

   A _____ also has fresh water.

2. A _____ has salt water.

   An _____ also has salt water.

3. _____ is part of the water cycle.

   _____ is also part of the water cycle.

C Look at the picture. Write.

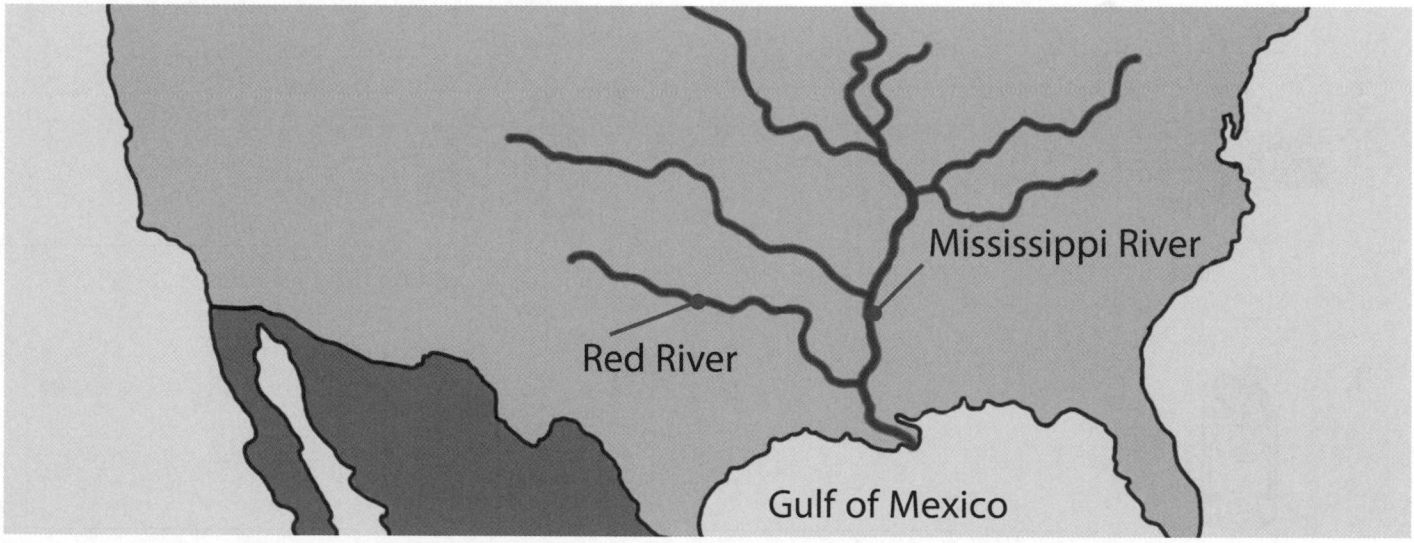

1. The Mississippi River has _____.

2. The Red River also _____.

3. The Gulf of Mexico _____.

63 The Environment

A Label.

bins	pollution	cardboard	exhaust	glass
smog	aluminum	litter	plastic	garbage

1.  _____

2.  _____

3.  _____

4.  _____

5. 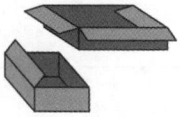 _____

6.  _____

7.  _____

8.  _____

9.  _____

10.  _____

B Write.

recycling picking up throwing away

1. She is _____ the garbage.

2. He is _____ litter.

3. He is _____ cardboard.

C Look at the picture. Write.

1. They are picking up _____.
2. She is _____.
3. He _____.

64 Space

A Write the words in the puzzle.

Across

1. 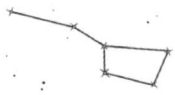
2. 
3. 
4. 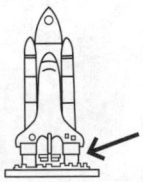
5. 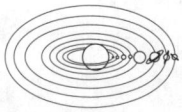
6. 

Down

7. 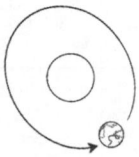
8. 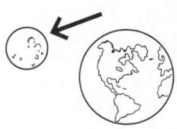
9. 
10. 
11. 
12. 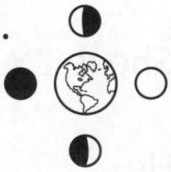

B Answer the questions.

star	planet	constellation

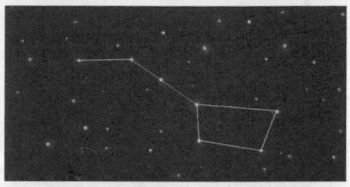

1. What is the sun?

   The sun is a _____.

2. What is the Big Dipper?

   The Big Dipper is a _____.

3. What is Jupiter?

   Jupiter is a _____.

C Look at the picture. Write.

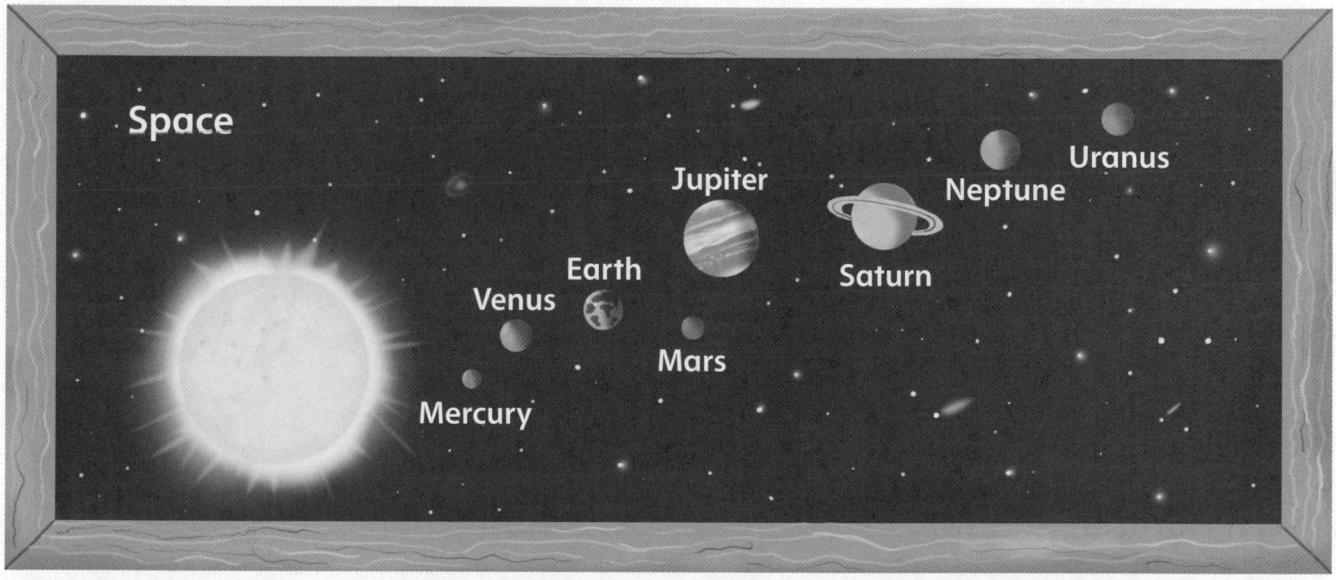

1. Saturn is a _____.

2. The Earth _____.

3. _____.

A Label.

boulder hill mountain rocks

1. 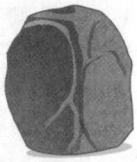

_____

2. 

_____

3. 

_____

4. 

_____

B Look at the diagram on page 154 of the *Dictionary*. Write *smaller* or *larger*.

1. A rock is _____ than a boulder.

2. A mountain is _____ than a hill.

3. A hill is _____ than a rock.

4. A boulder is _____ than a mountain.

C Complete the diagram.

gulf lake pond drops

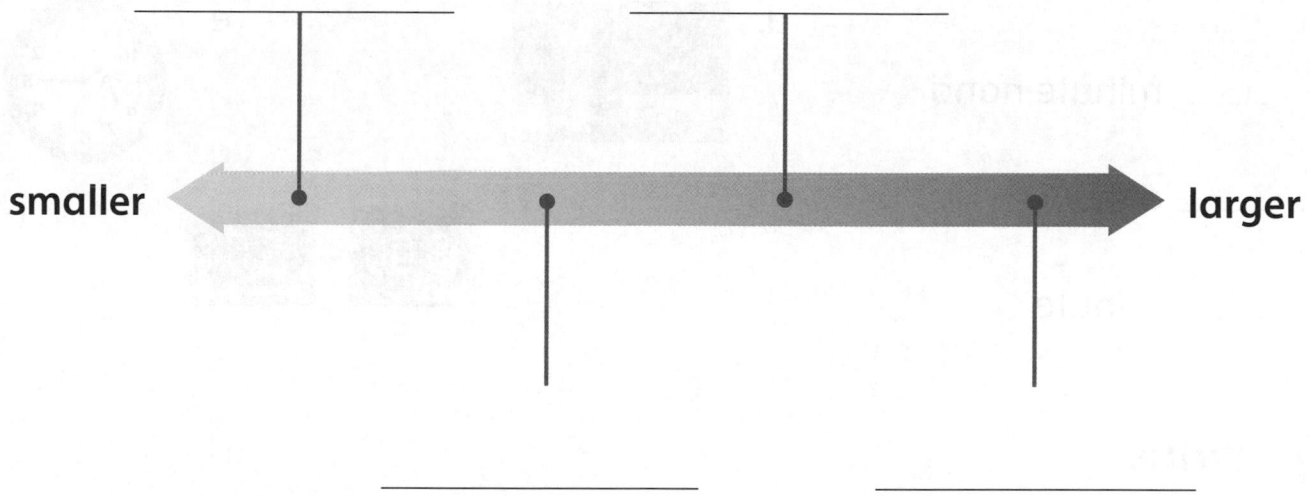

D Look at your diagram in C. Write.

1. A drop is smaller than a _____.
2. A gulf is larger than a _____.
3. A pond _____.
4. A lake _____.
5. _____.

65 Telling Time

A Match.

1. _____ hour
2. _____ p.m.
3. _____ hour hand
4. _____ minute hand
5. _____ a.m.
6. _____ minute

a. 

b. 

c. 

d. 

e. 

f. 

B Write.

twelve thirty | three fifteen | six o'clock | nine forty-five

1. 

_____

2. 

_____

3. 

_____

4. 

_____

C Write.

1. The _____ is on the twelve.

2. The _____ is on the three.

3. What time is it?

   It's _____.

D Look at the picture. Write.

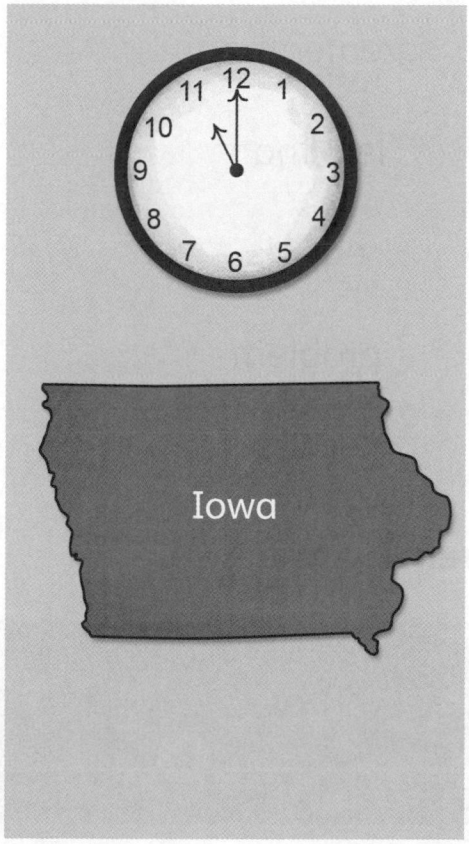

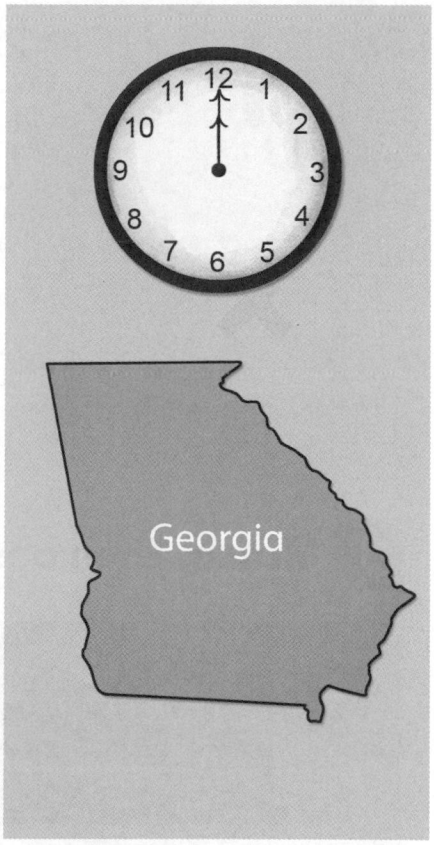

1. What time is it in Nevada? It's _____.

2. What time is it in Iowa? _____.

3. _____? _____.

66 Math Words

A Match.

1. 2+3=5
2. =
3. +
4. ×
5. ÷
6. −
7. >
8. <

add

subtract

multiply

divide

greater than

less than

equals

problem

B Match. Then answer the question.

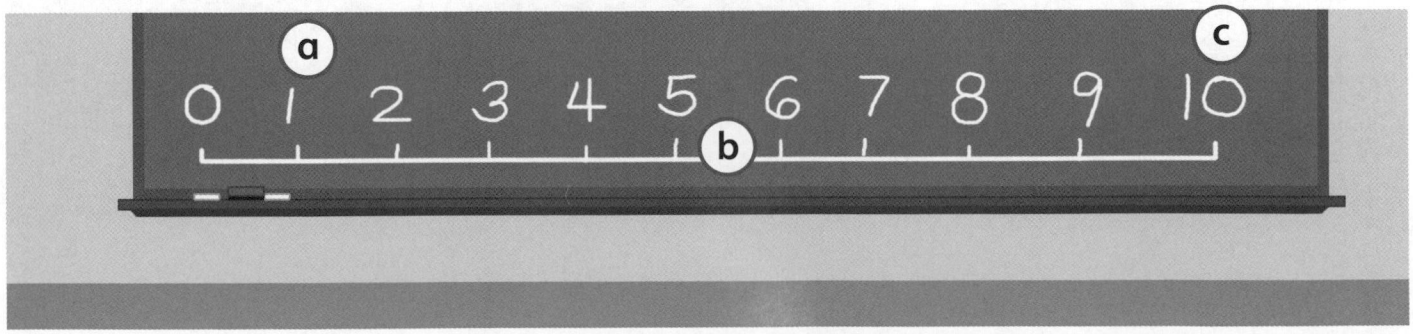

1. _____ odd number 2. _____ even number 3. _____ number line

C Write.

plus divided by minus times

1. nine _____ one $9 - 1$

2. eight _____ two $8 \div 2$

3. three _____ three 3×3

4. five _____ five equals ten $5 + 5 = 10$

D Look at the pictures. Write.

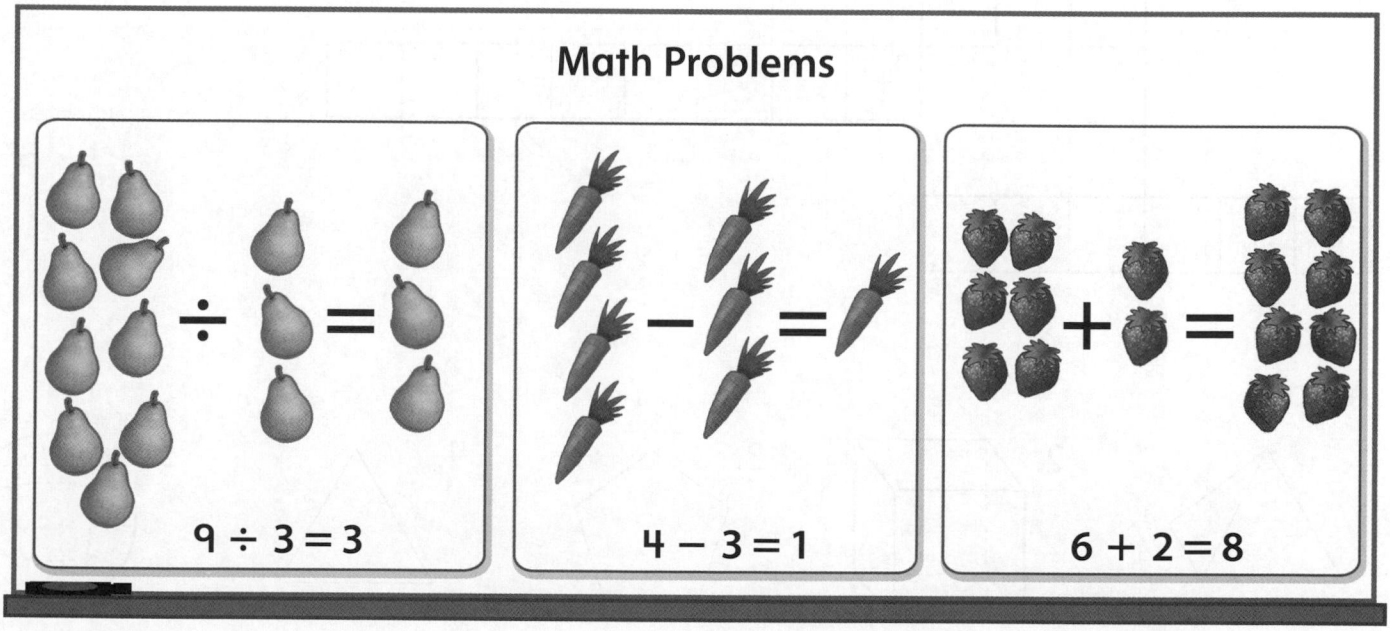

1. Nine divided by three equals _____.

2. Four minus _____.

3. Six _____.

67 Shapes

A **Write the words in the puzzle.**

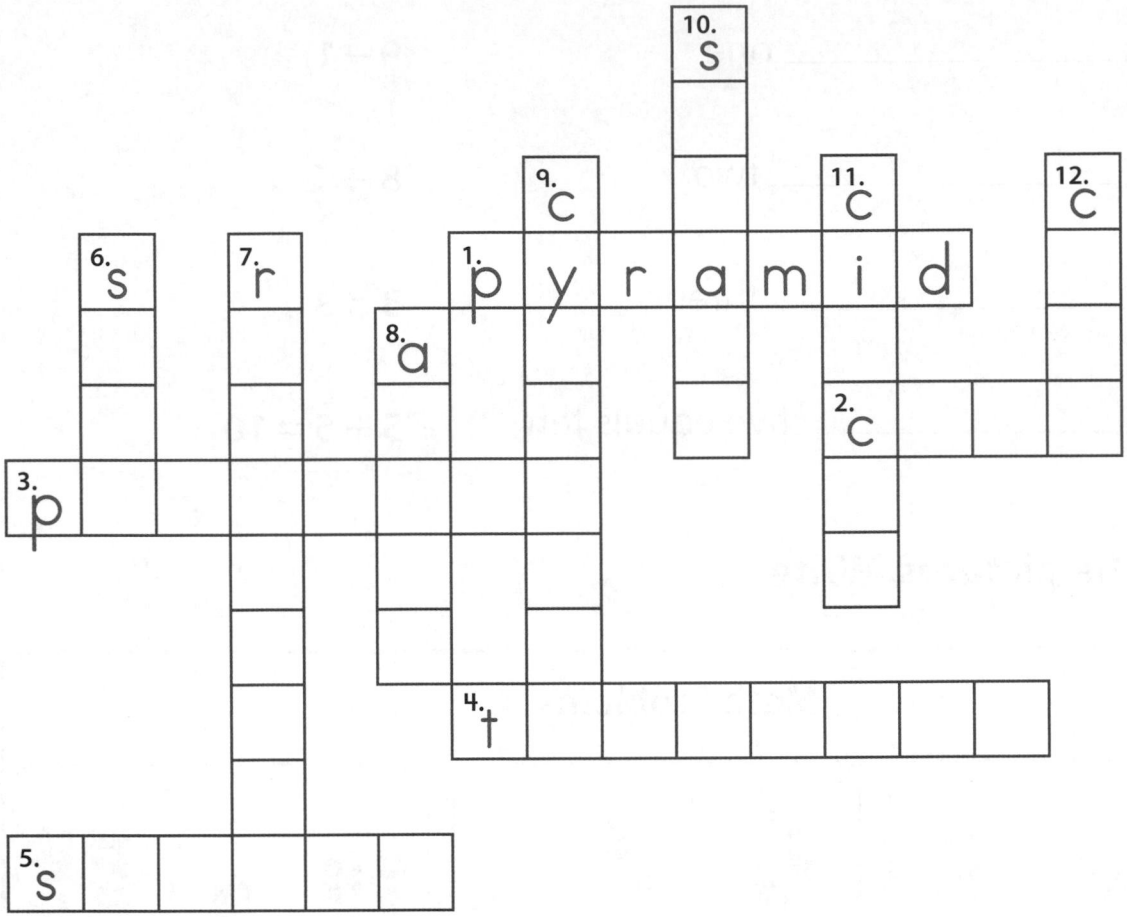

Across

1. 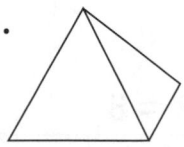

2. 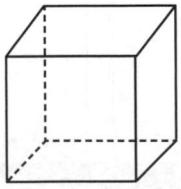

3. 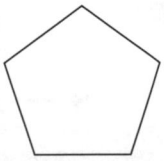

4. 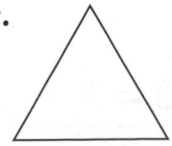

5. 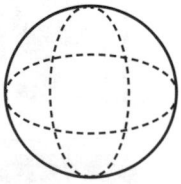

Down

6. 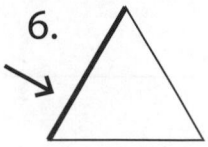

7. 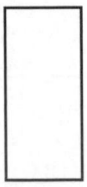

8. 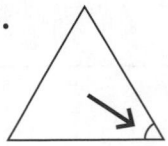

9. 

10. 

11. 

12. 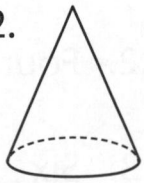

B Write.

three five six

1. A pentagon has _____ sides.
2. A triangle has _____ sides.
3. A cube has _____ sides.

C Look at the picture. Write.

1. A square and a rectangle have four _____.
2. A triangle and a cylinder _____.
3. A pyramid and a _____.

68 Fractions and Decimals

A Match.

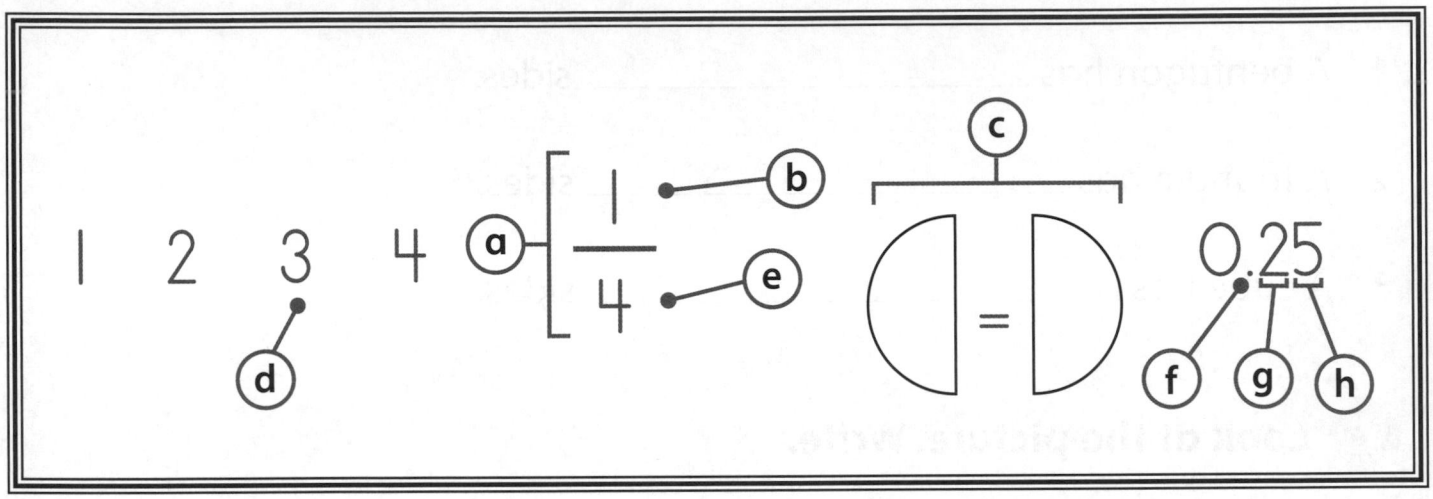

1. _____ fraction
2. _____ numerator
3. _____ whole number
4. _____ denominator
5. _____ hundredths place
6. _____ equal parts
7. _____ decimal point
8. _____ tenths place

B Label.

one half one third whole one fourth

1.  _____

2. 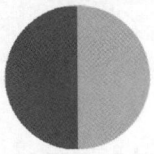 _____

3.  _____

4. 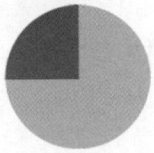 _____

C Write.

1. Does she have a _____ circle?

   Yes, she does.

2. Does he have one third of a circle?

   No, he _____.

   He has a _____.

3. Does she have _____ of a circle?

   Yes, she _____.

D Look at the picture. Write.

1. Clara has _____ of an orange.

2. Isabel has _____.

3. Andy _____.

69 Measurement

A Match.

1. _____ inch
2. _____ foot
3. _____ yard
4. _____ ounce
5. _____ cup
6. _____ pint
7. _____ quart
8. _____ gallon

a.

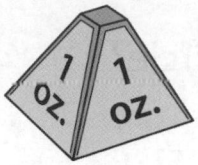

b.

c.

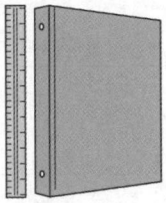

d.

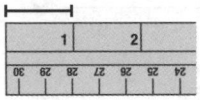

e.

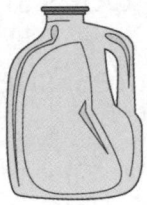

f.

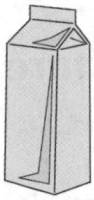

g.

h.

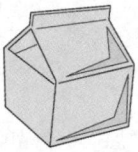

B Write.

liter centimeter gram meter

1.

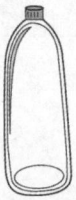

_____

2.

_____

3.

_____

4.

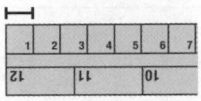

_____

C Write.

lighter longer larger

1. A yard is _____ than a foot.

2. A gallon is _____ than a quart.

3. Two ounces is _____ than four ounces.

D Look at the picture. Write.

1. Thirty centimeters is shorter than one _____.

2. A cup is _____ than _____.

3. Ten grams _____.

70 Money

A Match.

1. 
2. 
3. 
4. 

nickel

dollar

price

bills

penny

dime

coins

quarter

5. 

6. 
7. 
8. 

B Write.

save sell buy

1. 

_____

2. 

_____

3. 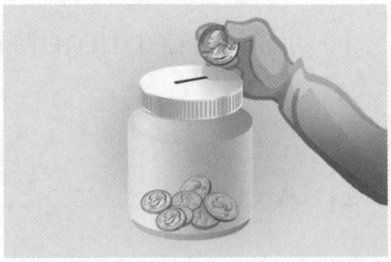

_____

C Write.

25¢ 100¢ 1¢

1. How much is a penny worth?

   A penny is worth _____.

2. How much is a quarter worth?

   A quarter is worth _____.

3. How much is a dollar worth?

   A dollar is worth _____.

D Look at the picture. Write.

1. Marta has one _____. It's worth _____.

2. Josh has three _____. They're _____.

3. Dan has _____ dimes. _____

   _____.

A Label.

whole one fourth one half one third

1. 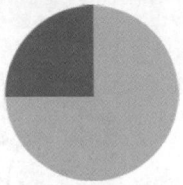

_____

2. 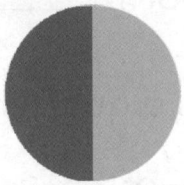

_____

3. 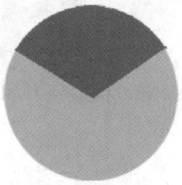

_____

4. 

_____

B Look at the diagram on page 168 of the *Dictionary*. Write *less* or *more*.

1. One whole is _____ than one fourth.

2. One fourth is _____ than one half.

3. One half is _____ than one third.

4. One third is _____ than one whole.

C Complete the diagram.

cup gallon pint quart

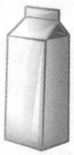

less

more

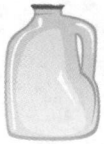

D Look at your diagram in C. Write.

1. A cup is less than a _____.
2. A gallon is more than a _____.
3. A pint _____.
4. A quart _____.
5. _____.